SEMEIA 45

THINKING BIBLICAL LAW

Guest Editor:
Dale Patrick

© 1989
by the Society of Biblical Literature

Semeia 45

Copyright © 1989 by the Society of Biblical Literature

All rights reserved. No part of this work may be reproduced or transmitted in any form or by any means, electronic or mechanical, including photocopying and recording, or by means of any information storage or retrieval system, except as may be expressly permitted by the 1976 Copyright Act or in writing from the publisher. Requests for permission should be addressed in writing to the Rights and Permissions Office, Society of Biblical Literature, 825 Houston Mill Road, Atlanta, GA 30329, USA.

ISSN 0095-571X
ISBN 1-58983-179-9

Printed in the United States of America
on acid-free paper

CONTENTS

Contributors to This Issue iv

Introduction
    Dale Patrick 1

The Problem of Ancient Israel's Prescriptive Legal Traditions
    Rolf Knierim 7

Studying Biblical Law as a Humanities
    Dale Patrick 27

Logic and Israelite Law
    Martin Buss 49

"Die He Shall Surely Die": The Structure of Homicide
in Biblical Law
    Peter Haas 67

Law and Philosophy: The Case of Sex in the Bible
    Tikva Frymer-Kensky 89

Rationale for Cultic Law: The Case of Impurity
    Jacob Milgrom 103

CONTRIBUTORS TO THIS ISSUE

Martin J. Buss
　Department of Religion
　Emory University
　Atlanta, GA 30322

Tikva Frymer-Kensky
　Reconstructionist Rabbinical College
　Church Road and Greenwood Avenue
　Wyncote, PA 19095

Peter J. Haas
　Department of Religious Studies
　College of Arts and Science
　Vanderbilt University
　Nashville, TN 37235

Rolf P. Knierim
　School of Theology at Claremont
　　and Claremont Graduate School
　1325 North College Avenue
　Claremont, CA 91711-3199

Jacob Milgrom
　Department of Near Eastern Studies
　University of California
　Berkeley, CA 94720

Dale Patrick
　Department of Philosophy and Religion
　Drake University
　Des Moines, IA 50311

INTRODUCTION

Dale Patrick
Drake University

Why would anyone want to study biblical law? That is a good question. Law is certainly not a burning issue to the college students who enroll in Bible courses. The textbooks used in such courses implicitly acknowledge as much by devoting only a very small percentage of the text to the subject.[1] I doubt that interest among Christian seminarians is much greater, judging from the course offerings of seminaries.[2] Even the community of biblical scholars finds law to be less interesting than other subjects—narrative, prophecy, psalms, even wisdom.[3]

A traditional Jew does have a ready-made answer: One studies the law because one is commanded to do so. It is God's will for His people, and one learns to serve Him by discussing it "when you sit in your house, when you walk on the way, when you lie down, and when you rise up" (Deut 6:7). This conversation is enlivened by the presence of past interpreters, who have constructed from the various and sundry rules of the Scriptural text a sophisticated, elegant conceptual system.

A conservative Protestant Christian would give a similar answer. Though the Christian had a less direct relationship to the law because the New Testament sets qualifications on its eternal validity, these words are still divine revelation and should yield both saving doctrine and instruction in obedience.

The typical undergraduate, however, does not fit the description of a traditional Jew or conservative Protestant, for there is no evidence of a demand among our students for in-depth study of biblical law. Moreover, critical scholars actively discourage the doctrinal approach to the text of Scripture which would arouse such a desire. Critical reflection seeks to historicize and humanize what is written, and when the origin of the law in divine revelation to Moses is disputed, the law's claim upon the reader's attention weakens substantially. It is difficult to sustain the will to immerse oneself in the laborious, painstaking study of a congeries of law which may be merely quaint and outdated mores and taboos.

The solution of the textbooks, and probably most courses, is to offer a relatively brief treatment of the Ten Commandments, historical observations about the publication of the lawbooks, and a few generalizations about values. None dig into the legal texts for their theology, anthropology, social philosophy, and ethics. The thesis of this volume is that we should be studying biblical legal texts precisely for these subjects. It is this sort of study which is meant by humanities.[4]

A Reply to Objections

Not everyone, of course, would define the task of biblical scholarship in terms of its role in academic teaching. The focus of our studies, they would say, is the formation of texts in their original environment. This has been the spirit of the critical enterprise for several centuries and should retain its primacy in the interpretation of the legal texts of Hebrew Scripture.

If this position is construed narrowly, our scholarship cannot be considered a humanities. It is essential to the humanities to study texts and history as sources of insight into the human condition. The texts are not artifacts of dead civilizations, but communications which require readers. The humanist must accept the role of reader him- or herself and induct one's students into this role as well.

Why should one prefer the humanistic model of scholarship over the scientific? Because it is more interesting, it involves the reader in a search for understanding, it releases the truth of the text for those in search for it. Historical critical scholarship is deadly when it is divorced from the art of interpretation.

The enterprise of critical scholarship can be understood in a different way. Each method of biblical study can be appreciated as a means of reconstructing a moment in the history of the text when it was a vital, living rhetorical exchange with an audience. For example, the form critical search for the original *Sitz im Leben* can be construed as the reconstruction of the moment when the text was oral, or first composed, to address an exigency in the life of the community. The text then entered the tradition and thereby into exchanges with subsequent generations. Each moment belongs to the meaning of the text as a communication to readers.

Members of traditional religious communities will perceive the project as a search for a substitute for religious interpretations. Whether one approves or disapproves of this sort of humanistic "apologetic," the very idea of a substitute implies that one kind of engagement with the text is to replace another. The text as a living word within a religious community will be set aside as no longer available to the student; in its place will be put a kind of counterfeit encounter with its ideas.

A reply is in order. To study biblical law as a system of thought does indeed change the kind of transaction between text and reader. Critical scholarship has consciously, systematically distinguished its approach to the Bible from that of religious communities, and the humanistic model proposed here belongs to the critical tradition. However, the study of legal texts for their conceptual system is quite open to theology and could enhance the religious appropriation of the texts.

It seems to me that there is a genuine analogy between the interpretation of biblical law as a system of concepts and principles and the Rabbinic discussions of divine law in the Gemara. The Rabbis were endeavoring to articulate and, where questions were open, to apply the concepts and principles informing the Torah and Mishnah. Their way of carrying on the discussion is more picturesque than ours, their assumptions about revelation are not compatible with humanistic interpretation, and their social setting is imbued with holiness, but the type of reasoning operative in their discussion is similar to what is being proposed.

The Story of this Volume

The authors of this volume have worked together over more than a decade in various program units of the SBL Annual Meeting devoted to biblical law. We decided that it would be worth the effort to put together a collection of studies that model the sort of scholarship we have been cultivating, a scholarship that aspires to transcend the analytical mode to gain an understanding of the subject matter and rhetorical transaction of the text.

There was no effort to impose a unity on the contributions by requiring a common subject, method, or text. Each scholar was encouraged to pursue his or her specific interests and long-range research projects. All that was asked was that the study be humanistic, that it interpret the text as a conceptual system which is a potential source of insight into the human condition.

If anyone of this group of independent-minded scholars had designed the whole, it would have a much different shape than it has. The present shape probably does not satisfy many of us. The reader should, however, be able to find studies to his or her liking.

Two of the essays—those by Knierim and Buss—examine the "logic" of law, while the others reconstruct the conceptual system which informs the biblical legal corpora. Knierim operates within a well-established critical methodology, form criticism, while Buss employs modern symbolic logic to exhibit its logical structure. Haas joins Buss in crossing disciplinary boundaries by applying the methods of cultural anthropology to textual exposition. Milgrom, Frymer-Kensky and I use whatever critical methodology and cross-disciplinary evidence we find helpful in expounding a subject. Although all of us assume the diachronic analysis of the legal texts, the studies are generally synchronic in character.

It was difficult to arrange the studies in order. One gains an appreciation for the problem of ordering confronting the ancient legal draftsman. Because each study has points of contact with every other, practically every combination is possible. Moreover, each possible order would communicate a different message to the reader. I decided to start with the essay which was most deeply rooted in the classical critical tradition, "The Problem of Ancient Israel's Prescriptive Legal Traditions" by Rolf Knierim. This essay exposes a serious gap in our form critical understanding of law; we have failed, he argues, to account for the *prescriptive* nature of the legal material preserved in the legal corpora of Hebrew Scripture. In essence, Knierim is saying that we do not really know what makes the judgments, commandments, and exhortations of our lawbooks law. This constitutes a definition of law for our volume, which is to say, that we do not know what we are talking about.

The next three studies constitute a group. My essay seeks to show how an interpreter can reconstruct the legal concepts and principles operating in a body of rulings. I want to justify the contention that biblical law can be studied as a humanities and offer a model for doing so. Buss examines the logical structure of the biblical legal system by means of a form of symbolic logic designed to analyze normative language. He demonstrates that various aspects of biblical law, particularly criminal and tort law, can be shown to be rational according to a particular system of logical analysis. Haas' study employs the analytical tools of cultural anthropology to recover the symbolic patterns by which ancient Israel understood the world. He uses the test case of homicide, which he correlates a deep pattern level with sacrifice.

Frymer-Kensky's study ranges over the whole of the biblical text for an answer to the question, how does the Bible understand sex? The sexlessness of the biblical God leaves something of a vacuum for the understanding of sex. Without a mythology or theology of sexuality, the Bible treats it primarily in law, where the question is one of controlling this volatile force. Though it is possible to discern some of the concepts and principles underlying these rules, the Bible does not provide, according to Frymer-Kensky, an adequate language for discussing and channeling this important aspect of life.

A significant portion of the laws governing sexual behavior belong to the category of laws of impurity. What are the concepts and principles which inform this category? Milgrom's essay shows that these rules constitute, collectively, a symbolic system which instructs Israel to eschew death and choose life. It seemed appropriate to conclude our collection of studies on this Mosaic note.

NOTES

[1] A survey of some of the more popular textbooks yields: Between 15 and 20 pages out of 528 in West; about 45–50 pages in Napier; Kuntz devotes about 20–25 pages out of 507; about 20–25 out of 643 pages in Anderson; and about 45 out of 609 pages in Gottwald.

[2] A random sampling of seminary catalogues yields: Of seven surveyed, three had two or three courses specifically on law, ethics (with law identified as a source), or books of the Pentateuch with law in them (invariably Exodus or Deuteronomy). The other four had only one course on any of these. Of course, introductory courses would include the law, and an exegesis

of a selected book could be of a book with law in it. However, every school offered more courses on prophecy and on wisdom than on law.

[3] One of the 57 program units of the SBL Annual Meeting is devoted solely to law, and a few others have papers on legal topics now and then.

[4] The study of law as a conceptual system is analogous to studying philosophical texts, differentiated by the different ways legal texts communicate the concepts and principles making up the system. I do not mean that we should look for an evolutionary scheme leading to a set of modern, liberal values, any more that I would recommend studying ancient or medieval philosophy for its "humanistic" teaching.

WORKS CITED

Anderson, B. W.
    1986   *Understanding the Old Testament*. 4th ed. Englewood Cliffs, NJ: Prentice-Hall.

Gottwald, N. K.
    1985   *The Hebrew Bible: A Social-Historical Introduction*. Philadelphia: Fortress.

Kuntz, J. K.
    1974   *The People of Ancient Israel: An Introduction to Old Testament Literature, History and Thought*. New York: Harper and Row.

Napier, D.
    1962/81   *Song of the Vineyard: A Guide Through the Old Testament*. Rev. ed. Philadelphia: Fortress.

West, J. K.
    1981   *Introduction to the Old Testament*. 2d ed. New York: Macmillan.

THE PROBLEM OF ANCIENT ISRAEL'S PRESCRIPTIVE LEGAL TRADITIONS

Rolf P. Knierim
School of Theology at Claremont and Claremont Graduate School

ABSTRACT

The essay addresses the problem of the legal prescriptions in the Hebrew Bible, i.e., the law-giving or "legislative" texts. It raises the questions of the nature of their forms, the persons or institutions (settings) involved in their creation, and their relationship to other legal institutions. Reviewing publications by Schulz, Liedke, Wagner, Boecker, *et al.*, it focuses on the death-penalty laws, the relationship between "legislation" and customary adjudication in the case laws, and on the relationship between law and ethos in the prohibitions. And it concludes with the question of the societal system in which ethos, adjudication and law-giving are interdependent.

Introduction

This paper focuses on the question of how the prescriptive legal traditions in the Old Testament can be explained. By "prescriptive legal traditions"[1] I mean the laws which set forth the rules or guidelines for the adjudication or arbitration of legal cases, and perhaps the rules of conduct. These "laws" are to be distinguished from those legal traditions that refer to the actual adjudication of cases. They represent a linguistic phenomenon which must be considered as generically different from the linguistic phenomenon found in texts that recount the adjudication of cases. A statement such as "if a person does so and so . . . the consequences shall be so and so" is different in kind from a statement such as *"because this person has done / you have done* so and so . . . you shall bear the consequences."

We may speak of the difference between legislative and adjudicatory language, and employ the word "legislative" to refer to prescriptive language regardless of whether or not that form of language presupposes the adjudicatory decisions of customary judiciaries. Such usage does not presuppose, as in modern times, legal systems in which the legislative, the executive, and judicial branches are institutionally separate *a priori*.

The methodological distinction between prescriptive or "legislative" and adjudicatory texts on the grounds of their different linguistic forms has a correlative in the distinction between different persons or groups who stood behind each of these linguistic forms. This methodological distinction is necessary unless we assume *e silentio* either that the circles who formulated the laws and the circles who adjudicated cases were identical, or that the functions of formulating laws and of adjudicating cases in the same circles were identical. Such assumptions, however, are unwarranted. While not necessarily separating legislation and adjudication we must, nevertheless, distinguish, functionally and possibly also institutionally, between the giving and the administering of law.

In this paper, I am concerned with the prescriptive legal texts as laws, and with the persons who formulated and gave them, and not with legal decisions pronounced in adjudicating processes, and the persons involved in those pronouncements. Form-critically, the two types must be clearly distinguished in terms of form, of genre, of function, and of setting.

It cannot be ignored that the scholarly literature on Ancient Near Eastern and Old Testament legal studies, which in my files alone exceeds 3,500 bibliographical entries, pays frequent attention to laws and lawgivers. But it is also true that frequently, especially in Old Testament studies, this side of the legal scenario is insufficiently addressed or in effect is collapsed into the adjudicatory side. This may be largely due to insufficient methodological clarification of the distinctively different notions pertaining to each side. Sometimes, even as we interpret laws or law-corpora, we speak about the administration rather than the prescription or "legislation" of justice, and about the adjudicators and their respective settings rather than about the law-givers and their respective settings.

This situation, however, presents a major problem. The major blocks of the Old Testament legal tradition represent prescriptive legal texts. As long as we do not recognize them in their distinctiveness, a significant part of ancient Israel's legal traditions, in fact, of the Old Testament literature itself, remains unexplained. This deficiency affects our understanding of specific laws, of the law-corpora, the history of the Old Testament law-corpora, and ultimately of the total framework of ancient Israel's legal institutions.

The scholar who addressed the problem of the laws as laws most programmatically and comprehensively more than forty years ago was M. Noth in his essay "The Laws in the Pentateuch." He determined as "the aim" of past research (!) and his own essay to define "the actual place of the [law] within the history transmitted by the Old Testament" (Noth:1). And he understood his study as a contribution to the interpretation of the OT literature. Noth's essay was ingeniously conceptualized and executed. To this day, it has remained the only one of its kind. The subsequent discussion developed for understandable reasons along the trajectory launched by A. Alt's "The Origins of Israelite Law." The task, however, as defined by Noth, remains. It must be resumed in light of the current situation.

This essay cannot discuss the whole development of the prescriptive traditions from the earliest beginnings in separate specific laws until the currently extant OT law corpora. Instead, I want to focus on some examples from recent research of specific legal prescriptions in the law corpora.

This paper raises questions more than it supplies answers. Perhaps it may stimulate discussion and further research. There is nothing programmatic about its selective use of publications. They serve, as many others could, as paradigms for demonstrating the problem. Absence of extensive bibliographical reference does not mean intentional neglect. I am just as much indebted to the corporate knowledge of the guild as anyone else. Whoever studies the literature on the sociology or anthropology of law, let alone the literature on law itself, is bound to realize how much can be gained from them for the studies in biblical law. Our discussion is far from sophisticated in this arena. Nevertheless, in order to avoid predetermining our understanding of the OT materials by systems possibly alien to them, it seemed to me for the time being important to advance our awareness of the questions arising from the materials themselves before they and the sociological perspectives are brought into a mutually critical dialogue. In this paper, aspects of modern sociology of law are, therefore, referred to selectively and with discretion, while the sociological and socio-historical implications in the discussion itself should be self-evident.

A. *First Example: The* môt yûmat *Laws*

The discussion will be confined to the interpretation of the difference between prescriptive—"legislative"—and adjudicative language in the works of H. Schulz, G. Liedke, and V. Wagner.

1. *H. Schulz*

a. For Schulz, the *môt yûmat* laws represent a genre *sui generis*, even among other forms of death-penalty laws such as the *lex talionis* and the various forms of casuistically formulated laws (192). Schulz calls this genre "*Todesrecht*" = *ius of death*.[2] Constitutive for this genre is the combination of the following components (79, 189): (1) the metrical structure of the sentences in which the substantive distinction between the legal case (*Rechtsfall*) and the legal consequence (*Rechtsfolge*) is stylistically compacted into one single sentence; (2) the legal case (*Rechtsfall*) is anchored in specific substantive prohibitive-norms (133) which themselves represent law (called by Schulz "*ius* of prohibition" = *Prohibitivrecht* [108, 190, *et al.*]); (3) the declaration of having fallen into or belonging to the sphere of death is expressed by the death-formula, מוֹת יוּמָת (which is to be translated "he belongs to (the sphere of) death" = "*er ist dem Tode verfallen*," and not, as usual, "he shall surely be put to death" [84]); and (4) the setting of this *ius of death*-genre is in a cultic or sacral juridical procedure.

The setting of this procedure had a history. Originally the procedure belonged to the tribe (99–112); not, however, to the family or clan! Then it was practiced by the town-communities. In this case, however, the local civil community had to reconstitute itself as a cultic congregation in order to protect itself from the consequences of bloodguilt (113–29). Or it was practiced at the Jerusalem sanctuary in a cultic trial in which the promulgation of the prohibitive-law and the *ius of death* were procedurally correlated (156). This trial proceeded according to a definitive structure the stages of which can be reconstructed from the compositional correlation of the prohibitions and the declaratory formulas found in Lev 18–20 (130–62).

b. At this point, we are specifically concerned with the differentiation between "legislative" and adjudicatory language in view of Schulz's thesis. The problem comes into focus at two points: his definition of certain prohibitions as *ius of prohibition = Prohibitivrecht*, and his understanding of the *môt yûmat* statements as declarations. As for the prohibitions, Schulz is certain that they represent a *legal* category which must have been promulgated in its prohibitive-form before and apart from *ius of death*-trials (*Todesrechtsprozessen*), though they may also have been recited in such trials as norms for the adjudication of cases.

c. This understanding of the legal nature of some prohibitions, however, requires that we explain them as law or "laws," that we explain the "legislative" notions in the act of their promulgation. We must also answer the questions as to how the "legislators" can be distinguished from the instructors of ethos, and whether the setting of such promulgation of prohibitive-law can be separated from the setting of the teaching of ethos, and whether the function of the promulgation of prohibitive-law and the function of the teaching of ethos in the same setting can be distinguished. The interpretation of these prohibitions as *Prohibitivrecht* (*ius* of prohibition) says only something about their legal nature; it does not explain the linguistic form of this legal nature, i.e., the people who formulated, gave, and proclaimed them as laws, and the distinctively legal context or setting of their proclamation. Such an explanation is called for precisely because of their definition as *Prohibitivrecht*. Though Schulz senses the problem (72), he is not able to provide an answer.

d. Schulz's definition of the expression מוֹת יוּמָת as "death declaration" intensifies the problem. What is a "declaration"? Apparently, it is an official, authoritative pronouncement by which a certain fact is established. It is a judgment rendered as a decision (141–42). Such judgments can establish a fact or its quality, an accusation made against a person, his/her guilt, and that he/she belongs to the sphere of death, among others. To be sure, the death-declaration is not a death-sentence (161; cp. however, his *"Todesstraf recht,"* 92). Together with the other types of declarations, it belongs to what we call the verdict.

One may ask whether the cultic trial reconstructed by Schulz and its formulaic language did not also have a stage after the death-*verdict* in which a death sentence determining the type of execution was pronounced (as in Lev 24:16aβb). One may further ask whether Schulz's death-declaration is not actually the declaratory pronouncement of a death-*sentence* itself (translated according to the customary "he shall surely be put to death") rather than the pronouncement of another verdict after the verdicts that establish guilt.

Decisive for Schulz's interpretation of the formula is the assumption that all declarations by definition belong to and are used in actual trials, i.e., in the *adjudication* of cases. Hence, the declaration מוֹת יוּמָת represents adjudicatory language because declarations belong to adjudication; and it is adjudicatory because it is identified as declaratory. It is not a death-*law* (*Todesgestz*). But he does not raise the question as to whether such formulaic declarations, including the entire participially formulated *môt yûmat* legal tradition, were also used in prescriptive legal (i.e., "legislative") settings. In other words, can a sentence (grammatically) labeled as death-declaration also be a death-*law* promulgated or described "legislatively"?

We have good reason to infer the existence of a distinctive prescriptive legal language and its respective settings. Methodologically, the assumption that declaratory language is by definition adjudicatory is not necessary, traditional as the assumption has been. In fact, we have reason to think that it is wrong.[3] There is not only evidence of a prescriptive-"legislative" promulgation of the *môt yûmat* statement in specific situations, there is the presence of the participially formulated death-statement in the context of the prescriptive legal corpora. We must attempt to account for the generically prescriptive nature of this and the other types of legal prescriptions in the legal corpora, and for their setting in oral or written events, situations, or procedures of legal prescription, i.e., "legislation." As long as the question is not addressed, the *môt yûmat*-"law" is, in my opinion, not satisfactorily determined, either generically or in terms of setting.

2. G. Liedke

a. For Liedke, the *môt yûmat* clauses following participle clauses are laws in the proper sense of the word. They represent legislation. More specifically, they belong to the genre of *apodictic law* ("*Der apodiktische Rechtassatz*," Liedke:101–53). In this law, the definition of the case is formulated not only in the participle form but also in the form of the relative clause, ... אִישׁ אֲשֶׁר (138–40). The tight connection between the participle form and the *môt yûmat* statement is not exclusive and, hence, not constitutive for the genre of the law. Nor is the death-penalty the only possible consequence. Apodictic law is neither exclusively death-penalty law nor exclusively expressed in participle form. Rather, the *apodictic* nature of this law is constituted by acts of sovereignty executed in legal promulgation by persons who have authority over a legal realm (125, 138). Such persons could be a *pater familias* in the patriarchal society, a king, or a military commander in chief. And the *"legislative"* nature of this law is constituted by the fact that the legal consequence, in fact, the entire law is *set forth before* the addressed case has happened (125).[4]

b. This law did not evolve from the judicial practice; it is not dependent on precedent judgments (129). Also, Liedke points out the difference between laws and judgments in the stylistic difference between the forms מוֹת יוּמָת and מוֹת תּוּמָת (direct address form; 128).

Furthermore, the apodictic legislative promulgation had its origin in the isolated sentence (*Einzelsatz*) referring to a specific, concrete situation (137). The series is not constitutive for the genre. Serialization reflects a secondary stage of development, abstracting from a case concretely focused on. It presupposes the experience of ever-repeated situations in view of which law is set forth generally. The series had its origin in the patriarchal family (cp. Exod 21:12, 15-17; Lev 20:11-13). Finally, the original setting of this apodictic legislation is definitely non-cultic.

c. Liedke's interpretation of the *môt yûmat* laws in participle form stands in sharp contrast to that by Schulz. Of particular importance is the implication that the distinguishable activities between legislation and adjudication were in the hands of the same authorities. This implication suggests a picture of society—and not only of the patriarchal family—in which the administration of justice, without separating a legislative from an adjudicatory *branch*, distinguished between legislative and adjudicatory *functions* in the same hands.

Naturally, one will have to ask which role the townships played in such a picture, whether the same correlation was also the case behind the apparently priestly texts such as Leviticus 20, and what the relationship was between the non-cultic origin of this apodictic law and a possibly cultic setting. These questions were not pursued by Liedke. Their clarification remains a desideratum.

3. *V. Wagner*

a. According to Wagner, the participially introduced *môt yûmat* laws represent generically a series of ten crimes (19-21) that draw the death-penalty. Accordingly, Wagner calls them *"Die môt yûmat-Reihe."* The series, which no longer exists in the OT texts as a whole, must be reconstructed from Exod 21:12; 15, 16, 17; 22:18; Lev 20:10, 11, 12, 13, 14. This reconstruction requires also the reconstruction of the text in Exod 21:16, and in all the Leviticus passages where the case is presently stated in the >*îs* >*aser* relative sentence form rather than in participle form.

The series identifies criminal delicts (23) by its use of the expression מוֹת יוּמָת, a technical term for "death-sentence" (27). It reflects *ius* of death-penalty (*Todesstrafrecht*, 30). It is forensic in nature (26), based on legal norms the violation of which calls for adjudication (31). It is not based on ethical norms. The crimes themselves referred to in the series were not related to Yahwism or the cult. They reflect the nomadic society. Accordingly, there series belonged to the repertoire of the ANE legal collections and, hence, also to the courts (29), especially to the intertribal judiciary of nomadic law (30). It functioned orally as a repertoire for the courts (29).

b. Wagner's reconstruction of his series is highly doubtful, if not totally unwarranted.[5] Of particular interest for our discussion is the fact that Wagner does not develop any distinction between the prescriptive or "legislative" and the adjudicatory implications in the interpretation of his series. He comes close to this distinction when associating the series with the ancient law collections, but he immediately blurs it by relating the series also to the courts, i.e., to an adjudicatory function and setting. In the same vein, he talks about its *"Memorierform"* (29) but fails to explain who composed, formulated, prescribed, and taught what was to be memorized and possibly used by courts as law.

Wagner does discuss how the *legal* nature of these laws can be explained as a collection of *laws prescribed "legislatively."* Unfortunately, the use of the word "forensic" (26) contributes nothing to such a clarification because "forensic" means at least also, if not predominantly, "pertaining to, connected with, or used in courts of law" (*Oxford English Dictionary* 1973). Nor does the definition of these laws as technical terminology for a death-*sentence* (*Todesurteil*) clarify anything as long as one does not distinguish between death-sentence as a *"legislative" definition* and as an *adjudicatory pronouncement*.

4. Conclusions

a. Linguistically, we have every reason to distinguish between a prescriptively or "legislatively" formulated phrase and the form of a pronounced judgment. Accordingly, we have reason for distinguishing between the setting of "legislative" activities and the setting of adjudicating activities even if both types of activities were at times or under certain conditions carried out by the same persons. Or should we assume that laws were *by definition given*—not recited! (to whatever extent this happened)—in conjunction with trials, at the same places where and at the same times when trials were in process, and always by the same persons who conducted trials? Even so, we would still have to account for the distinction between prescriptive and adjudicating language.

b. More importantly, we would have to develop a sociological model in which the primary symbiotic institutionalized interwovenness of both forms of language can be made plausible. Such a model has not been developed so far except, perhaps, by Schulz. However, such a primary model does not seem to be promising. The alternative to it would have to be a model in which the nature of the prescriptive or "legislative" language of our text is taken seriously in its own right, i.e., one that takes seriously the *generic* nature of its forms, its settings, and functions. When this task is done, we should be in a better position to interpret the relationship between law-*giving* and the *adjudication* of law in the administration of justice, and to develop a more comprehensive picture of the history of ancient Israel's legal system.

B. Second Example:
The Casuistically Formulated Laws

I presuppose what is generally assumed: that the case-law reflects the tradition of the adjudication or arbitration of civil or criminal cases which is common to the Ancient Near East; that it is based on precedents and, hence, primarily customary law and non-cultic in origin;[6] and that its basic form consists of two components, a protasis describing the case, and an apodosis defining the consequence.[7] I want to discuss the question whether the case-laws are *reports of* decisions or *prescriptions for* decisions. Specifically: Do the *formulations* of these laws represent reporting or prescriptive language? Are these formulations protocols of cases adjudicated in court, or are they prescriptions intended as a *basis for* the adjudication of cases in court?

It seems to me that this question must be clearly distinguished from the controversially debated question whether these corpora are laws or decisions (See Grothus:1). That debate centers around the difference between laws in the sense of newly enacted legislation not based on precedents, and laws based on customary decisions.[8] Even if or where the laws are based on customary decisions, the question still remains whether they are formulated as court-decisions or as prescriptions or proposals for court-decisions.

The question on which I am focusing must also be distinguished from the generally assumed fact that the *description* of the cases and the consequences in the laws points to their relationship with the adjudication of cases in customary law. The fact that they describe cases and consequences does not at all affect the question whether what is described is formulated prescriptively as the possibility of a future event, or as a record of a past event. Likewise, our question must be distinguished from the question whether the legal regulations (the apodoses) in the laws are *proposals for arbitration* which may or may not be accepted by the litigants, or whether they are *legally binding*, i.e., whether the legal regulations reflect remedial law to be negotiated between the litigants, or punitive law imposed by a third, the judicial, party in authority.[9]

Once our question is brought into sharp focus, the answer seems clear at least for the ANE laws. These laws are to be distinguished from court records, the decisions of which are formulated quite differently.[10] They are formulated generally, envisioning any and every case of their sort, and not specifically referring to a singular case listing pertinent data specifically. And they look forward to a possible event, but do not report already adjudicated cases. They aim at permanence (Paul:9). They are legal prescriptions (Paul:41,114) or prescribed legal norms (Paul:3; Preiser:36). In this sense, they represent legislation.

As for the ANE royal laws, this interpretation is virtually self-evident inasmuch as the king is also the supreme lawgiver and not only the supreme judge (So Grothus:17–18 for the Hittites). However, this interpretation is important in a more fundamental sense unless one assumes that the legal norms prescribed in case-law form were rooted in royal legislation exclusively, an assumption that is unwarranted. Therefore, we have to ask where the matrix of this prescriptive legal language[11] as a genre *sui generis* was. Who were the persons who formulated it, and why? Or, how can their function as formulators of it be understood, in distinction from other functions which they may have had? In what sense did they function as formulators of law or as lawgivers institutionally?

An answer to these questions that points to the judiciary as the matrix of the case-laws is unsatisfactory. This answer does not explain the transformation of adjudicatory into prescriptive language; for even if the persons accountable for both types of language were the same in some legal system, or if the matrix of both types of language were the judiciary only, we still would have to assume that these persons functioned differently and at different moments when functioning as lawgivers and as judges, and we still would have to distinguish between legislative and judicial activities in the judicial setting and/or process.[13] As for the king, we have reason to assume that the laws issued by him were intended to be administered in adjudication not only by himself, but by other judges as well.

Likewise, our question is not answered with reference to the *contextual notions* of casuistically formulated law which points it out as remedial law (Cp. Paul:116, with reference to R. A. F. MacKenzie). The characterization of the content and judicial context of these laws is no substitute for the explanation of the matrix of the legislative nature of their language. Paul, quoting MacKenzie, says: "It is a crystallization of jurisprudence. . . ." (116). We should like to have a clearer picture of this "crystallization."

I submit that the sociological interpretation of the prescriptive legal language of the case-laws as a type of language in its own right deserves specific attention beyond the interpretations given so far. Moreover, unless we assume that they owe their existence to acts of writing law-collections, the task has to involve the search for the oral matrix of individual case laws or short series of them.

The particular problem addressed in this paper can also be observed in the OT studies on the case-law. Liedke's otherwise penetrating discussion is a case in point. The thrust of his argument is to show that the OT case-laws were closely related to the adjudication of cases in courts, and that they in fact grew out of arbitrating decisions practiced in the customary judiciaries. For him, the adjudication strictly consisted of proposals of and for arbitration, while the decisions functioned as precedents for future trials. Liedke does realize the difference between what I call adjudicating and prescriptive "legislative" language, between a judgment and a law (e.g., 19). He knows that, strictly speaking, a decision and a law are not the same. On p 55, quoting one of Koschaker's examples, he says that such a decision was transformed into a legal rule ("*Rechtsregel*").

But then he says:

> "*Die so entstandenen kasuistischen Rechtssätze sind also ihrer Herkunft nach nicht gesetztes Recht; ihre Autorität beruht auf Herkommen und Sitte; sie sind Gewohnheitsrecht. Die Rechtskorpora ... sind ... (Zusammenstellungen gewohnheitsrechtlicher Entscheidungen).*"[12] Or: "*Während der kasuistische Rechtssatz konzentrierter und abstrahierender Bericht eines Rechtsverfahrens ist und hinter ihm nur die Autorität des Einverständnisses aller Beteilgten steht, ist der apodiktsche Rechtssatz von der höchsten Autorität eines Rechtskreises gesetzt*" (124–25).

In these formulations, Liedke actually misses the point in his own awareness of the differences between a judgment and a law. It is the question as to what constitutes a law as law once it is transformed from the formulation of a decision into a prescriptive statement. Liedke does not explain why such transformations happened, who made them, how the persons who made them functioned, and what the function of these new formulations was meant to be. Why were they necessary at all if, as Liedke correctly states (56), the knowledge of the precedent decisions alone could make the way to the court superfluous?

When Liedke says that the case-laws are not "law set forth" (*gesetztes Recht*) because their authority rests on custom, he apparently assumes that prescribed or "legislated" law is by definition only newly enacted law, and that no prescribed law can ever by based on customary law. Such a methodological assumption, however, is indefensible. It only prevents us from interpreting the forces that stand behind the *transformation* from customary decisions to legal prescriptions, i.e., from interpreting the event of transformation itself and, ultimately, the nature of the legal prescriptions themselves.

Similarly inconclusive is the argument quoted from pp 124–25 which says that the case-law is a concentrated and abstracting report (*Bericht*) of a trial backed up only by the consensus of all involved, in contrast to the apodictic law which is enacted by the highest authority of the legal realm.

This argument is unclear in at least three regards. First, it does not sufficiently distinguish between a decision in court and a law. A case-law is not a "report of a trial" only. To whatever extent it reports or describes, and whichever of its two parts is reported or described, it is a reporting or describing *prescription*.

Second, Liedke's argument does not distinguish between the *consensus* behind a decision in court and the *consensus* behind a legal prescription. We should distinguish between the consensus of those who reach a decision in court, and the consensus of those who stand behind the formulation of a case-law. The difference between these two kinds of consensus is clearly that decisions in court are confined to the arbitration or adjudication of specific cases momentarily before the court, whereas case-laws, on the basis of the tradition of such decisions, reflect the communal consensus on the arbitration or adjudication of such cases in the future.

In formulating the laws and collecting them in written corpora, the community by consensus seems to intentionally bind its future court decisions to rules laid down permanently and for its courts. The community seems intentionally, as far as those laws that are formulated are concerned, to consent to *law* as the future basis *for* the courts, and no longer on the ongoing transmission of decisions by the courts. The development from decision to law is in part reversed into and in part accompanied by a development from law to decision. Thus, the legal community becomes a legally prescribing community, a community based on law, instead of and/or in addition to being a community based on customary adjudication only. What evolves is communal legislation as a separate institutional process in the whole of the legal system. And the linguistic transformation from court-decisions to legal prescriptions appears to be a correlative to the transformation or diversification of, in our case, ancient Israel's legal system itself.

Third, Liedke infers that the *authority* of the decisions and/or the laws is based on the consensus of all involved in a trial, including the defendants. The case-trials were trials involving arbitration.

Related to this inference is Liedke's assumption of the quite different authority standing behind the apodictic laws. The authority of apodictic laws is absolute because it rests on "the highest authority of a legal realm," whereas the authority of case-decisions or of case-laws is relative because it demands the consensus of all, including defendants.[14] If such a consensus is not reached, the arbitrating proposal falters. In such a situation, the community has only the authority to arbitrate by proposal. And decisions or case-laws are in principle nothing more than proposals.

One must ask, however, whether this model covers all the situations that came before the communal courts. It seems that in cases involving the remedy for damages or the adjudication of crimes once a defendant is convicted, the community had very much the authority to impose or dictate a decision, regardless of the agreement of the defendant and regardless who was entitled to execute the decision. In such cases, the decision would not have been proposed by the community and made by the disputing parties. Rather, it would have been dictated by the community itself. And it would have had absolute authority, just as an apodictic law had, precisely because the deciding community represents "the highest authority of the legal realm" itself.

Therefore, the relative or absolute authority of a community's decision does not seem to depend on a trial as a case-trial, or simply on the community's consensus, let alone on the agreement of a convicted defendant. It seems to depend on the *type* of case before the court, i.e., the *arbitration* of, e.g., a dispute with claims and counterclaims or a business transaction on the one hand, or the *adjudication* of a damage done or a crime on the other hand.

The same seems to be true for the absolute or relative authority of the laws themselves. Their case-law form can scarcely be taken as proof that they were meant as nothing more than guidelines for *proposals* in arbitration which left the involved particies at liberty to accept them or not.[15] This casuistic form says nothing about the authority of the laws or the kind of authority which the legislating community ascribes to itself in them.

This also means that the word "casuistic" must not be understood as "relative," in opposition to "apodictic" understood as "absolute" or "categorical." "Casuistic" is the expression for the focus on a case in distinction from other cases. Whether the expression is descriptive of prescriptive, authoritative, categorical, or relative, depends on factors other than the expression itself. These factors are to be sought primarily in the *kinds* of cases addressed by the laws: disputes and negotiations subject to arbitration, or damages involving remedies and fines as well as crimes involving punishment.

In this respect, it is not coincidental that the Covenant Book deals with delicts, which suggests that its definitions of legal consequences intend to be dictated or imposed by the adjudging community, and not negotiated by the opposing parties. And inasmuch as these laws reflect the transformation from customary decisions to laws, from adjudication to legislation, they signal the intended reinforcement of the adjudicatory authority and of the legal authority of the tradition of customary decisions for future adjudication.

Reflecting on the possible origin of the Book of the Covenant, H. J. Boecker (143–44) suggests that "the preservation and promulgation of the so-called divine law" was the task of the "judge of Israel," somebody like Samuel. It "was the judge's business ... to reinforce the jurisdiction of the local court by assisting in the verdicts; the purpose of this was to raise local verdicts to the status of law." In what sense should the judge have assisted in the verdicts of the local court? If on the basis of or with the help of *already formulated* law, the assistance would have helped in keeping the verdicts in line with established legal prescriptions. This interpretation reveals something about the application of the law to local court-procedures, but nothing about the matrix of the law itself which preceded the conception of the Book of the Covenant (on the origin of its conception, see p 144). If the judge assisted in the verdicts by transforming verdicts into laws, the "judge of

Israel" would function as a law-giver, as one who "raised the local verdicts to the status of"—supralocal?—"law," which is more than and different from assisting in verdicts. The question that must be answered about this thesis is: is the surmise that the case laws owed their existence to individual supralocal judges preferable to the alternatives?

Shalom Paul clearly speaks of the case laws in terms of legal prescriptions (101) and legislation. And in quoting Speiser he emphasizes the "setting" in which the Book of the Covenant "originated." His own surmise is a theologico-cultic setting which is, in my opinion, correct. Despite his call for the determination of the setting, however, Paul himself explains neither the matrix of the case laws nor the matrix of the corpus in a sociologically perceptible way. The problem remains with us.[16]

C. Third Example: The Prohibitions

In the Judeo-Christian tradition the prohibitions were, together with all other legal forms, subsumed under Divine or Mosaic Law. Albrecht Alt had persuaded many scholars that the prohibitions represented one of several particular forms of genuinely Israelite law, of apodictic law. Since E. Gerstenberger, it has been clear for many that they belong to the tradition of ethical instruction and not to law at all. Their form (no case-consequence pattern; direct address form instead of neutrally formulated statements) is different from typical legal case-law formulations; coupled with Gerstenberger's thesis that their original setting was in families or clans, the evidence seems to speak against legal, especially "legislative," settings. Even when occurring in cultically determined contexts, the prohibitions are thought not to be laws but ethical or cultic instructions administered through the cult.

It seems to me, however, that the question should be re-opened. Clearly, no prohibition can any longer be assumed to be a law by virtue of being a prohibition. But is it equally clear that no law can be expressed as a prohibition? We have reason to pursue this question, for neither the inclusion of all prohibitions into law, nor the exclusion of all prohibitions from law provides any longer a defensible model for our understanding of the Old Testament prohibitions.

I cannot discuss here the problem of the value-systems of societies in which a society's perception of normative order and justice represents the basis for the development of its morals and laws, and their interdependence. This problem can be studied systematically in Anthropology of Law, Sociology of Law, and History of Law. Suffice it to say that the awareness of this problem is crucial for our subject. Our interpretations of the relationship of prohibition and law in ancient Israel affect our selection of anthropological and sociological models of Israel, and our preconceived models affect our interpretation of the relationship of prohibitions and law. One understanding critically affects the other.

Since we nowhere in our ancient sources possess a systematic treatment of Israel's world-view, we have to proceed to discuss the relationship of prohibition and law itself, yet with constant critical awareness of the implications for our model of Israel's anthropological and sociological self-understanding. For such a discussion of the *relationship* of prohibition and law, it is important to notice from the outset that this relationship is by definition mutually neither exclusive nor inclusive.

In the pursuit of this subject, I turn to a section in G. Gurvitch's discussion which is particularly pertinent for our problem. As part of the "specific marks" of "law ... or jural regulation or legal social control" which are "distinguished from all other kinds of social regulation or control (moral, religious, aesthetic, or educational)" (44), Gurvitch lists the following characteristics:

(a) "The determined and limited character of jural commandment versus the unlimited and infinite character of other commandments, especially of strictly individualized moral exigencies. For instance, the commandment, 'thou shalt not kill,' has a different sense in law and in morals. In law, there are set cases in which one can, others in which one must kill (self-defence, war, executions, etc.). In morals, the prohibition may include not only all these cases, but also all acts which might become indirect causes of death, from a refusal of aid in dangerous circumstances to hurtful words which might shorten somebody's life" (44).

(b) "Bilateral or more precisely, multilateral character of jural regulation, constituting its imperative-attributive structure, as opposed to the unilateral *imperative* character of all other types of regulation. The imperative-attributive structure of all manifestations of law consists in an indissoluble link between the duties of some and the claims of others. This link is possible only in jural regulations in connection with the determined and limited character of its commandments which permit the application of a common measure to related claims and duties" (45).

(c) "The indispensability of a [social guarantee] of effectiveness of law giving assurance for a real correspondence of claims and duties and showing itself in the necessity for all law to be [positive], that is, to derive its validity from normative facts. It is normative facts which unite the characters of authority, not identical with rules, and the efficient social guarantee ..." (45).

(d) "Not necessarily requiring its execution by precise exterior constraint, law admits the possibility of being accompanied by this constraint, while moral and aesthetic requirements exclude the possibility of execution by this constraint, and religious and educational commandments exclude the possibility of its having any precise or fixed character.... Let us clearly distinguish external and precise constraint from the more general phenomenon of sanction, and sanction from social guarantee. All law accompanied by constraint presupposes law not accompanied by such constraint but which is fit to justify the former.... In any case, all law is sanctioned by the reprobations of the social milieu in which it is violated, but not all law is accompanied by constraints" (46).

The meaning of these descriptions of the characteristics of law, related to our specific problem, can be summarized as follows: first, a prohibition or command can be law, just as it can be an ethical imperative, but it is not by definition a non-law; second, law has an imperative structure the legal nature of which depends on the societally regulated adjudicability of duties of some and claims by others, i.e, on the social guarantee of that imperative structure; and third, laws do not have to be formulated casuistically. They can, but do not have to be accompanied by definitions of consequences ("constraints").

This picture should not come as a surprise. Generally speaking, commands and/or prohibitions have not been excluded from the definition of law in legal history. The Oxford English Dictionary defines law first of all as "a rule of conduct imposed by authority." Nor has such exclusion been the case in many recent studies in Ancient Near Eastern and Old Testament law. For example, R. Yaron points to four "terse commands" which he calls "apodictic," in sections 15–16, 51–52 in the Laws of Eshnunna, and to such commands in paragraphs 36–40 and 187 of Codex Hammurabi (145–46). One cannot conclude that these formulations are non-legal because no consequences are mentioned. On the contrary, one can only conclude that the mentioning of consequences is not an indispensable feature of a legal prescription. In fact, CH 36 and 37 show the intrinsic correlation of apodictically and casuistically formulated laws.

H. J. Boeker seems to point in the same direction when, discussing the "differently structured parts" of the Book of the Covenant, he says: "The oldest Old Testament code, even in its basic form and content, thus becomes a paradigm of Old Testament law" (141). Later on he raises "the question . . . whether we can strictly speak of law in this connection. The answer is no if in law we include detection, judgment, sentence and punishment; the answer is yes if by law we understand legal principle or maxim" (201).

For A. Phillips, the question of the relationship between ethical and legal prohibitions can be clearly decided: "The only adequate definition of a crime is that conduct which the state prohibits" (2). A prohibition issued by *the state* is *a law*, hence the title of Phillip's book. *Legal* prohibitions involving crimes are state-laws. Our only problem with this understanding is: How can we know which of the Old Testament prohibitions — including the Decalogue which "constituted ancient Israel's pre-exilic criminal law code given to her at Sinai" (1) — were issued as state-laws?[17]

Of particular interest for our question is once more H. Schulz who, as I mentioned before, regards his *ius of death (Todesrecht)* as based on an antecedent *ius of prohibition*. Schulz supports his judgment that some prohibitions are legal by citing Kantorowicz (5, n. 2) to the effect that *ius (Recht)* should be conceptualized in such a way as to include even the most primitive notions of legal thinking. Following Kantorowicz, Schulz says: "*Man wird m. E. in den Prohibitiven doch so etwas wie Recht zu sehen haben.*" (5).

He then analyzes the legal nature of some nine or ten prohibitions specifically (6–61). His criteria for determining their legal nature are the substantive congruency of the violations expressed in the *môt yûmat* laws and of those prohibitions, and the circles of persons adversely affected by the violations (13).

This exposition by Schulz seems to me to point in the right direction. I may not go for his *Todesrecht*, but I am inclined to go for his *Prohibitivrecht*. One does not have to assume "primitive notions of legal thinking" in order to appreciate the existence of legal prohibitions in ancient Israel, even in the clan setting. In fact, the clan itself as a setting of prohibitions proves nothing concerning their legal or ethical nature. It was itself both a legal and ethical entity (on law in the clan, see Schulz:72). Especially, the idea that prohibitions may very well represent the *basic* matrix of legal development, particularly in ancient societies, deserves much more study than it has received so far. It may be that it is in the prohibitions in which the emergence of law out of traditional ethos, or in which the transition from traditional ethos to law becomes most directly visible.

Schulz' work should be expanded in two respects: On the one hand, we should venture into the realm of such prohibitions that can be identified as legal even though their violation required less than the death-penalty. On the other hand, we should ask whether the methodological basis for identifying legal prohibitions can be broadened and refined by isolating—in Gurvitch's sense—further clues for clear correlations between prohibitions and their adjudicatable societal control, control especially of the interdependence of duties by some and claims by others.

If this analysis of the issue is correct, the total field of the prohibitive traditions in the Old Testament and the Ancient Near East would have to become subject to a new orientation in our research. This orientation would have to be guided by questions such as: Which prohibitions can be determined as legal and which ones can be determined as ethical or otherwise? Where, when, and why in the course of history did ethical prohibitions become law? And ultimately: What was the interdependence of ethos and law in ancient Israel's social fabric?

NOTES

[1] This paper is a slightly revised version of a paper originally submitted to the consultation on Biblical Law and Comparative Studies at the meeting of the Society of Biblical Literature on December 12, 1982, in New York City. I am indebted to Henry T. C. Sun, senior Old Testament Ph.D. student at Claremont, and my research associate at the Institute for Antiquity and Christianity, for editorial assistance.

[2] The word *ius* is used here for "*Recht,*" in distinction from "law" = "*Gesetz,*" and "a/the law(s)" = "*ein/das (bestimmte) Gesetz*" or "*die Gesetze.*"

³ Cp. now the Ph.D. dissertation (Claremont Graduate School) by R. R. Hutton (1983).
⁴ Liedke: *"Der apodiktische Rechtssatz" ist "von der höchsten Autorität eines Rechtskreises gesetzt. Nicht ein Präzedenzfall wird [erzählt], nach dem man sich, wenn ein ähnlicher Fall eingetreten ist, richten kann, sondern: bevor der ins Auge gefasste Tatbestand sich ereignet hat, wird von der ubergeordneten Autorität des Königs, Heerführers usw die Rechtsfolge festgesetzt."*
⁵ The textual reconstruction is problematic; the selection of ten from a larger reservoir conflicts with the selection by Schulz of a cultically oriented series (cp. 79–80). While Liedke regards the >îs >ašer form, together with the participle form, as apodictic law without saying whether one emerged from the other (140), R. Yaron defined the >îs >ašer statements on different grounds as a "proclamation-form" which may occasionally have been legal in nature but not so necessarily, in Yaron (137–53).
⁶ On the "complete separation" of law, moral rules, and religious orders in the Ancient Near East, of types that "are never combined in a single corpus," cp. Paul:8.
⁷ For a convenient summary of the variety of forms, see, among others, Paul 112–15.
⁸ The widespread assumption that the casuistically formulated laws reflect law based on customary decisions does not seem to be universally correct. In the Hittite laws, e.g., the regulation in nineteen paragraphs explicitly distinguishes between "formerly" and "now," thereby indicating newly enacted legislation. Cp. Götze:188–97; Grothus:8–11; also, among many others, Preiser:17, who refers to the *reformatory* nature of the collections
⁹ With regard to the question, the quite different nature of cases addressed, and the quite different structure of the ancient judiciaries as well suggest anything but a uniform picture.
¹⁰ Cp. *Ancient Near Eastern Texts*:212–23; Haase:119–27.
¹¹ With "matrix" I mean, sociologically, the institutional setting, as distinct from "origin" in the historical sense, as from the Sumerians, according to Paul:116.
¹² For his Proclamation-form, e.g., R. Yaron finds the setting in life in "1) the actual life of the market, 2) the law courts, . . . 4) the naked command of a ruler, 5) the sphere of the proclamation," thus referred to by Paul:115. The problem with this list is that it does not distinguish between—in this case—the proclaiming activities proper and other activities. While the cases 4) and 5) identify the proclamation-activity as such, the cases 1) and 2) identify its *place* only, without distinguishing this activity from other activities in the market and the law courts.
¹³ Liedke:56, including a quotation from R de Vaux.
¹⁴ The basic model for this interpretation reflects L Köhler's scenario. However, Köhler's model, ingenious as it was, has quite inappropriately become universalized and applied for the interpretation of all kinds of cases adjudicated in the gates. Köhler's own case-study, from the Book of Ruth, involved a business-transaction for which the consensus of all is self-evident even if one assumes a legal dispute. The situation is quite different if one considers the adjudication of cases involving damages done or criminal acts. Such differences in the kinds of cases are not considered by Liedke at all. As long as they are not critically discussed, an interpretation of case-law as law of arbitration alone is unsubstantiated.
¹⁵ This aspect ought to be clearly distinguished from the question of whether these laws ever played, or were meant to play, a role in actual adjudication. Law meant to function in adjudication as proposal is one thing; proposed law meant to be adopted for adjudication is quite another.
¹⁶ Concerning the relationship of law and juridical process, M. Clark certainly points in the right direction when saying that "the actual relationship of casuistic law and juridical process, once both are firmly established, was more reciprocal and complex. The court did not simply apply the statute nor did the statute simply put into writing past decisions and in every case derive from an actual court-case" (112).
¹⁷ For an extensive review of Phillips' book, see Jackson:54ff.

WORKS CONSULTED

Alt, Albrecht
    1966   "The Origins of Israelite Law." Pp. 79–132 in *Essays in Old Testament History and Religion*. Oxford: Basil Blackwell.

Boecker, Hans Jochen
    1980   *Law and the Administration of Justice in the Old Testament and Ancient East*. Minneapolis: Augsburg.

Clark, Malcolm
    1974   "Law." Pp. 99–139 in *Old Testament Form Criticism*. Trinity University Monograph Series in Religion 2. San Antonio: Trinity University.

Götze, Albrecht
    1955   "The Hittite Laws," Pp. 188–97 in *Ancient Near Eastern Texts Relating to the Old Testament*. Princeton: Princeton University.

Grothus, Jost
    1973   *Die Rechtsordnung der Hethither*. Wiesbaden: O. Harrassowitz.

Gurvitch, Georges
    1974   *Sociology of Law*. London/Boston: Rutledge and Kegan Paul.

Haase, Richard
    1965   *Einführung in das Studium Keilschriftlicher Rechtsquellen*. Wiesbaden: O. Harrassowitz.

Hutton, Rodney R.
    1983   "Declaratory Formulae: Forms of Authoritative Pronouncement in Ancient Israel." Dissertation, Claremont Graduate School.

Jackson, Bernard S.
    1975   *Essays in Jewish and Comparative Legal History*. Leiden: E. J. Brill.

Köhler, Ludwig
    1956   "Justice in the Gate." *Hebrew Man*. Nashville: Abingdon.

Liedke, Gerhard
    1971   *Gestalt und Bezeichnung alttestamentlicher Rechtssätze*. WMANT 39. Neukirchen-Vluyn: Neukirchener.

Noth, Martin
    1966   "The Laws in the Pentateuch: Their Assumptions and Meaning," Pp. 1–131 in *The Laws in the Pentateuch*. Philadelphia: Fortress.

Paul, Shalom M.
1970 *Studies in the Book of the Covenant in the Light of Cuneiform and Biblical Law.* VTSup 18. Leiden: E. J. Brill.

Phillips, Anthony
1970 *Ancient Israel's Criminal Law.* New York: Schocken Books.

Preiser, Wolfgang
1969 "Zur rechtlichen Natur der altorientalischen 'Gesetze'." In *Festschrift K. Engisch.* Frankfurt/Main: Klostermann.

Schulz, Hermann
1969 *Das Todesrecht im Alten Testament.* BZAW 114. Berlin: Alfred Töpelmann.

Wagner, Volker
1972 *Rechtssätze in gebundener Sprache und Rechtsatzreihen im israelitischen Recht.* BZAW 127. Berlin: Walter de Gruyter.

Yaron, Reuven
1962 "Forms in the Laws of Eshnunna." *Revue International des Droits de l'Antiquité* 9:137–53.

STUDYING BIBLICAL LAW AS A HUMANITIES

Dale Patrick

Drake University

ABSTRACT

The title states the thesis of this article: Biblical Law can and should be studied as a humanities, which is to say, a coherent and comprehensive system of thought. We can ally ourselves with certain current legal philosophies to overcome the non-humanistic understanding of law; within biblical legal scholarship we can carry on the tradition of Moshe Greenberg and J. J. Finkelstein. Finkelstein's study, *The Ox That Gored*, provides a model for recovering the scheme which informed legal rulings. We can identify and trace out the concept of causation as it is applied to cases of injury and death, the metaphysical scheme of a hierarchy of being, and the principle of the unquantifiability of human life. These concepts and principles are communicated by the ordering and shaping of specific rulings to be discovered by inferential reasoning, the sort of reasoning a judge would employ to determine the application of the law to a particular case.

Perhaps the suggestion that the law is a repository of a culture's reigning metaphysics, anthropology and ethics seems rather far-fetched. Law is perceived by the average citizen as a technical enterprise involving the application and manipulation of rules and evidence. And law students are taught to regard their profession in this way; history, philosophy and ethics are only marginal to their curriculum.

The regnant philosophies of law in English-speaking countries aid and abet the divorce of law from theology, philosophy and the other humanities. Legal positivism defines law as the "will of the sovereign,"[1] while Marxists define it as a tool of the ruling classes to keep the masses in subjection.[2] Both of these models regard the body of rules and decisions which constitute the law to be in force only because they were imposed by authoritative bodies.

There is something of a movement afoot to reinstate the study and practice of law as a humanities.[3] Such a view would define law as normative because it embodies the theological, metaphysical, and ethical convictions of the legal community. The authorities who decide cases and enact statutes would be regarded as agents of the community's will. Evidence of that is found in the fact that precedents and statutes are supported by reasoning from concepts and principles which claim allegiance apart from the interests of the power-groupings of society.

The proposal to study biblical law as a humanities finds this movement to be a natural ally. Perhaps we can even contribute to its intellectual elaboration and cultural advancement. The study of biblical law could exemplify a mode of interpretation which exhibited biblical law as a coherent conceptual system. In the process, it could disclose those values and principles of our own law which derive from this tradition[4] and do constitute a coherent, compelling understanding of the human condition.

Recovering Biblical Law as a Conceptual System

Unfortunately, the scholarly climate of biblical research has not been particularly conducive to the understanding of biblical law as embodying theology, anthropology, ethics, and social philosophy. Several factors have worked to deflect our interest and undermine our confidence in its sophistication: (1) Critical biblical scholarship has developed agendas for the study of law which concern its origins and transmission, not its thought. (2) Modern scholarship is biased against the capacity of the legal minds of antiquity to think with sophistication and system.

(1) The first great break-through in higher criticism focused on identifying documents or sources and locating these in the history of Israel. The identification and location of the lawbooks and collections of Exodus, Leviticus, Numbers, and Deuteronomy played a significant role in the evolution of source criticism. Wellhausen's great classic, *Prolegomena to the History of Israel*, devotes nearly one half of the argument to the dating and placing of law in a developmental scheme.[5] His efforts were concentrated on those practices and institutions which distinguish a given work from others and which might locate the work in a particular period of history and/or stage in the development of Israelite law.

There was nothing in the source-critical agenda that ruled out the study of the legal concepts and principles operative in a given lawbook or underlying all of them. However, the intellectual proclivity of the source critics seems to have blinded them to the systematic character of legal thinking. The diachronic mode of explanation dominated the critical mind of the 19th century and continues to exercise an inordinate influence, whereas judicial reasoning is essentially synchronic.

Form criticism and tradition history shifted scholarly study of law away from the origins of specific legal texts and the practices promulgated in them. These methods helped to free us of an implicit understanding of ancient law on the model of legislation. Lawbooks and series were now understood to belong to traditions which antedated their publication by centuries. Form criticism taught us to recognize the style and structure of legal formulations and to relate these to social settings,[6] while tradition history taught us to see the material in a variety of continuities.

Neither form criticism nor tradition history, however, have encouraged the study of law as an intellectual system. Form criticism tends to fix its sights on the verbal formulation of legal statements, while tradition history is still wedded to genetic accounts of texts. One suspects that the practitioners of these methods have not been trained in law and/or have come under the influence of defective accounts of legal reasoning.[7] We have gained a great deal of knowledge of the history of the texts, of specific provisions, of drafting patterns, and of social settings, but our standard critical methodologies have furthered our knowledge of the law as an intellectual system only marginally.

(2) Biblical scholars have tended to regard biblical law as "primitive" in its ideas and devoid of system. For some reason, an explanation of a ruling which sees some magical and superstitious idea at its root seems more plausible than an explanation based upon a "modern" legal concept. As to system, Henry Sumner Maine still speaks for many critical scholars when he portrayed ancient law as a congeries of vague principles and concrete rulings.

Though such a characterization would appear to be the conclusion of years of experience, it is actually an *a priori* interpretive stance. An interpreter cannot simply look at an ancient text and decide whether it is consistent or not. Rather, one must consider what the gaps, order, and reasoning mean. If one assumes that the legal doctrine taught in the texts is limited to the explicit verbal formulations, each considered in isolation, any conceptual scheme will escape one's notice. If, on the other hand, one projects him- or herself into the role of a judge seeking an answer to a legal issue, the formulations will be read for the principles and concepts applicable to the issue; a comprehensive, consistent system will emerge in the process of interpretation.[8]

How can one confirm the superiority of one or the other interpretive posture? Probably no decisive test can be designed. However, hermeneutical principles may resolve the impasse. The legal texts would be better texts if they constituted a comprehensive, consistent system of principles and concepts, and interpretation should be committed in principle to interpreting texts as the best texts they can be. If the search for a conceptual system regularly yields inconsistencies and gaps, then we will have to conclude that the legal texts of the Torah are not very good, or are best interpreted as something other than law. If, on the other hand, a sophisticated, profound conceptual system can be constructed which accounts for the legal statements of our texts, the conceptual, synchronic mode of interpretation will be vindicated.

The position I am advocating was enunciated nearly thirty years ago by Moshe Greenberg in his contribution to the Kaufmann Jubilee Volume (1960). In that essay he argued that scholars should study biblical and ancient Near Eastern law "as an expression of underlying postulates or values of culture" (8). The interpreter should put him- or herself in the place of the ancient jurist or draftsman, who would have perforce read its legal statements as constituting a consistent, relatively comprehensive system (7).[9]

While Greenberg's thesis was discussed, the time was not yet ripe for it to have the impact on interpretation that it deserved. Our situation may be different, for confidence in genetic explanations of the text has been shaken by synchronic approaches to narrative and poetry. The interpretation of law as a system of concepts and principles is comparable for this genre to the poetics of narrative and poetic literature.

It should be mentioned that Greenberg's proposal did bear some fruit in the last few decades. There have been a number of scholars who have been working diligently over the years to work out the conceptual systems governing ancient Near Eastern and biblical law. I would single out David Daube, J. J. Finkelstein, Shalom Paul, Y. Muffs and one of the contributors to this volume, Jacob Milgrom, as exemplary practitioners of conceptual interpretation.

Finkelstein's Goring Ox

In the rest of this essay I want to demonstrate the conceptual exposition of biblical law. I am not offering a definitive method for interpreting law as a humanities, for I do not believe that any set method is desirable. Our procedure should be methodical and our argumentation well-reasoned, but we should be free to pursue the leads the text offers and our imagination opens.[10] We are not seeking an uncontroversial interpretation of the legal material, but an interpretation which makes it the best text it can be. This is a matter of intuition and judgment, and it will be incumbent upon me to persuade you that the interpretation set forth is indeed the best understanding of the text. Your task is to hold me to my promise, to examine the text with me and assess the quality of the interpretation.

We need a specific case to focus our investigation. I propose the passage in the Book of the Covenant on the goring ox (Exod 21:28-35). I choose this passage because it is the launching pad for J. J. Finkelstein's fascinating and profound exploration of biblical law (5-47). In this section I will review his interpretation of the legal reasoning embedded in this specific set of casuistic remedial laws.[11] In the following sections I will trace out a number of concepts and principles found in this set into other laws and beyond.

Finkelstein understands this "law" to be entirely theoretical. It is found in Eshnunna ##53-5, indicating not that it was a common problem (which is unlikely), but that it was a traditional case for the legal draftsman's art (15-21). It offered interesting challenges to the application of legal theory. With that in mind, the differences between the ANE treatment and that of Exodus are quite instructive.

There are a number of features in the passage which arouse one's curiosity: (1) The ox that kills a human is destroyed by stoning. (2) When the owner is guilty for not restraining a known gorer, he is liable to execution. (3) The owner who is liable to execution can be ransomed. (4) The law reiterates its ruling for the goring of a child. (5) An exception is made of the goring of a slave. (6) The responsibility of a pit owner interrupts the goring of one ox by another.

Why is the ox that gores a human to death destroyed by a method otherwise associated with capital punishment? The method of killing clearly suggests the concept of punishment, not just the destruction of a dangerous beast.[12] The animal is being treated as "guilty" of an offense. The question is, what is it guilty of?

The odd idea that an animal, which obviously lacks the equipment to make moral choices, can be treated as guilty has attracted much scholarly speculation. Not infrequently one hears that the passage reflects a "primitive" conception of guilt, either that the animal is thought to have a moral will or that guilt is completely objective, i.e., requires no intention to kill. Even Brevard Childs, who is generally a judicious interpreter, believes that Exod 21:28 "seems to reflect a more primitive conception of guilt, as indicated by parallels from other cultures (Frazer, *Pausanias' Description of Greece*, London, 1898, II, pp. 370ff. . . .)" (473). Such a judgment evidences an overconfidence in historical-critical reconstruction according to some scheme of cultural evolution. Childs rejects an explanation which fits the passage into the conceptual structure of biblical law in favor of a much more speculative linkage to alleged parallels.

That explanation is offered by Finkelstein: the ox must be destroyed because it has violated the hierarchy of being (God-humanity-animals-plants) (26–29). This is not guilt in the moral sense. If it were, we would expect a trial of the animal in which questions of provocation, etc., were raised. Moreover, execution would be by the avenger of the blood. The violation is, rather, metaphysical, and "punishment"[13] for violating the metaphysical order does not require subjective guilt. It is comparable to a human inadvertently encroaching upon sacred space.[14]

So, far from being primitive, the law of the goring ox has a sophisticated understanding of causation and evidence. The ox which caused the death is an agent of its owner. The owner's responsibility for his agent's action is proportional to his capacity to predict such behavior. If the ox's behavior had evidenced a penchant to gore and he has not taken adequate precautions, its characteristic behavior can be imputed to the owner's will. The most difficult question for the court is whether the owner knew of the ox's inclinations. After the fact, charges would likely be thrown around rather wildly, so the court requires that testimony be given of prior warning (86–87).

Why is the ox owner liable to execution? The penalty seems completely out of proportion to the offense. Accidental homicide is never treated in this way elsewhere in biblical law (see Exod 21:12–14, etc.). Moreover, the ancient Near Eastern parallels are much more "rational," exacting a fine from the owner.[15]

One could again appeal to a concept of "primitive guilt." However, Finkelstein offers an explanation much more congruent with biblical law: biblical law refuses to assign a monetary value for the life of any victim (29–32). The only possession the owner has equal to the value of the victim's life is his own.

The law-giver, however, does not really intend that the death penalty be exacted. Rather, the stipulation is designed to initiate negotiation over monetary payment. It is the living person who has a price put on his head. The aggrieved family has been granted virtually absolute power over the person responsible for their plight. The law-giver has preserved the principle that a victim of homicide not be assigned a monetary value and yet facilitated a monetary exchange; in the process, the aggrieved party has been granted superior power in negotiations with the offender.

Children and slaves have been singled out for special mention. The case of children is covered to exclude the possibility of exacting the life of the owner's child for the life of the victim (Finkelstein:32–35). Such rather literal applications of the *lex talionis* is known in the ANE (Hammurabi ##229–30), though not in the laws of the goring ox. Our law-giver simply took the opportunity to state a principle of biblical law.

The death of a slave is an exception to the rule that no monetary value can be assigned to a victim. Evidently the slave is not being accorded the status of human, but of property. This is out of keeping with the rest of the Book of the Covenant, which elsewhere refuses to recognize a metaphysical hierarchy within the human race (see below).

Why the discussion of the goring ox interrupted by the subject of liability for an open pit? Daube suggests that 21:35–36 are an amendment to the law, placed at the end of the section rather than contiguous with the law that it amends (85–89, 96–98). While this is possible, it is unlikely. There is no reason to believe that it is an amendment.[16] Finkelstein's explanation is more interesting: the subject has changed. An ox killing an ox is essentially different from an ox killing a human. Humans belong to a different metaphysical order than oxen. An ox killing another ox is indeed quite similar to a pit killing an ox; both are simply cases of loss of property. It is probable, in fact, that the drafter of the law interrupted the killer ox laws in order to avoid any suggestion of an analogy (36–39).

Concepts and Principles of Biblical Law

The virtue of studying the set of provisions governing a goring ox is that its very marginality and peculiar twists of reasoning afford a glimpse into the concepts and principles of Israelite judicial reasoning. Simply to understand its rulings, we had to reconstruct the intellectual system "behind" it. Now we are ready to expand the scope of our study to cover provisions which are not so marginal or peculiar in reasoning. We can trace out the legal doctrine identified in the law of the goring ox through provisions of killing, injury, and beyond. On occasion we will even venture outside the lawbooks to examine narratives which exemplify the same concepts and principles.

There are good reasons for assuming that the concepts and principles informing the provisions governing a goring ox are common to the legal tradition. The first is consistency. Most legal systems aspire to treat like cases alike. English Common Law embodies this principle in the structure of judicial reasoning; the task of a judge in the Common Law is to work out a scheme of concepts and principles which explains and justifies all the relevant precedents of the case before the bar and then to apply it to the case (Dworkin 1977:105–30 and elsewhere).

One might doubt that biblical jurists were as sophisticated and systematic as the Common Law ideal. Such a judgment evidences, I believe, a modern prejudice (Maine 1861). If the very idea of law involves the principle that like cases should be treated alike, one should assume that ancient drafters of law intended a consistent system. It is appropriate for us to assume their capacity to attain such consistency until discrepancies and lacunae force us to conclude otherwise.

The drafters of biblical law had an additional reason for seeking consistency, *viz.*, theological consistency. Biblical law is understood to be the will of YHWH, Israel's God. Since the unity and consistency of God was a fundamental principle of Israelite theology, the drafters of that law would surely take care to exemplify His unity and consistency in law and the interpreters of the text would have understood the lawbooks as calling for the kind of reasoning that constructs such a consistent unity.

There is another reason to expect consistency in Israelite law, the principle of exhaustiveness. It has long been noted that biblical lawbooks do not cover all possible cases on a given topic for all the areas of judicial action (for example, see Moore:251–62). This would seem to contradict the necessity of a legal system to bring all judiciable cases under a set of concepts and principles. That too is implied by the principle of treating like cases alike.

Given the seeming contradiction, we must ask how the biblical lawbooks functioned. There are good reasons to believe that they did not have the force of binding codified law (See Patrick 1985:198–200, Finkelstein: 15–21). I would suggest that they were designed to inculcate the concepts and principles of Israelite law for judges and the community at large. A selection of cases would be sufficient to set forth this intellectual system, and in that sense it is exhaustive.

Now we can trace out the concepts and principles identified in the set of provisions governing the goring ox through other sets of provisions and narratives. We will begin with causation.

The Concept of Causation

Remedial law involves the determination of who and/or what caused a particular state of affairs to come about and a classification of the action of the responsible parties. The legal concept does overlap the scientific, but in addition to identifying the physical cause[17] the court desires to assess responsibility and classify the act. In the case of the goring ox, the court is concerned with assessing the responsibility of the owner. The owner has the duty of protecting the community from the acts of his charge. To prove neglect of duty, biblical law requires the owner's knowledge of the dangerous propensity of the beast.

To appreciate the subtlety and resilience of the concept of legal causation, it may be instructive to observe how it disregards a commonly accepted doctrine of modern philosophical ethics. The doctrine in question is that matters of fact are of a different order than judgments of value. According to this view, it is fallacious to describe a state of affairs and then derive a moral rule or value from it. It is often stated in terms of "is" and "ought": no "ought" can be derived from an "is."[18]

The legal concept of responsibility synthesizes "is" and "ought," fact and value. Responsibility involves moral categories, for a person is judged according to whether he or she acted as one ought to. The very classification of actions, say the distinction between accidental, negligent, and felonious homicide, is defined in terms of ought and ought not. The classification system is, nevertheless, descriptive. When a trial occurs, the examination and evaluation of the evidence leads to a classification of the actions of the parties, which is at the same time a "moral" judgment, a judgment as to innocence or guilt.

In cases of homicide, the primary principle of classification is willfulness. A person should be held accountable for acts which he or she should or should not have done. There is no accountability if the person could not have known that he or she should or should not have acted in a certain way or if the person could not have for physical (or perhaps psychological) reasons acted differently. If knowledge and capability can be established, the person can be held culpable for untoward actions.

In cases where a person is the physical cause of death or the initiator of a chain of causes resulting in death, the act is classified according to willfulness or intentionality. Biblical law recognizes precisely the same fundamental distinction as our legal system does, *viz.*, between murder (felonious homicide) and accidental homicide. The provisions of the Book of the Covenant read (Exod 21:13–14):[19]

> Accidental Homicide: "he did not lie in wait for him, but God let him fall into his hand."
> Felonious Homicide: "a person willfully attacks another to kill him treacherously."

The first definition would seem to leave a lot of leeway; a person who killed in a momentary passion might seem to be exonerated of murder. The second, for its part, seems to require too much premeditation and violence. I doubt, however, that this impression is accurate, for other passages tend to hold actors to a rather high standard of responsibility.

There are two other biblical passages enunciating the distinction, Deuteronomy 19 and Numbers 35. Deut 19:4–5 describes accidental homicide as unintentional and without enmity, and then illustrates it with an example of an occurrence which is clearly accidental. V. 11 continues to describe murder in rather melodramatic terms. Num 35:16–21 looks for evidence of the intention to kill in the means used; weapons, lethal objects, even hands, constitute such evidence. The drafter has to admit, however, that accidents occur when such means are evident, so the court has to ask how the means happened to strike its lethal blow (vv 22–23).[20]

Any legal system worthy of the name must add refinements to cover grey areas between murder and accidental manslaughter. What if a person killed another in self-defense? Or in a fight? Or as result of a legally entitled beating? We have provisions in the Book of the Covenant dealing with each of these.

We do not find the expression "self-defense" in biblical legal texts, but at least one provision employs the concept. In the section of the Book of the Covenant covering theft of livestock (Exod 21:37–22:4), the law-giver considers the question of killing a thief in the act of breaking in (22:1–2). If the thief is killed at night, the killer is not guilty of murder; if in the daytime, he is. The principle guiding this ruling is: killing is justified to protect oneself and family, but not to protect property. If it were legitimate in the protection of property, there would be no distinction between night and day. The ruling assumes (as does English Common Law) that the intruder who uses the cover of darkness is more dangerous; he may be armed, he can lurk in shadows and attack, his identity is unknown; even his intentions are uncertain. During daylight hours, the thief can be avoided, his armaments known, he can be identified and apprehended; the owner, too, could reasonably expect a cry for help to be heeded by neighbors. Of course, if the thief were brandishing a weapon and threatening to harm the owner or his family, the case would be altered.

Injury and death resulting from fights present complicating factors. A fight involves putatively willing participants; if both fight fairly, each must accept whatever he or she suffers as the consequences of his or her action.[21] The Book of the Covenant treats cases of injury to participants and bystanders. In a case where one fighter is injured by another (21:18–19), the inflictor of injury is not charged with a felony ("he is clear"). Nevertheless, he must pay for the convalescence of the injured. The description of the case specifies the means of injury—"a stone or his fist." Neither of these is normally a weapon, so the court must assume that the striker did not intend to kill (which would be attempted murder); they were means resorted to in the heat of the fight. A stone, though, is dangerous and should be considered "unfair" fighting; why a fist is listed along with it is puzzling. In any case, I think that we can surmise that "striking a blow" makes the inflictor of injury responsible for healing; if the injury had resulted from falling on a stone while wrestling, the one who was injured should have to pay for his own healing.

A few verses later the law-giver treats the case of injury to a bystander (21:22–25). The bystander selected for consideration is a pregnant woman. The law-giver appears to be primarily concerned to rule on injury causing abortion. "Punishment" for causing an abortion by fighting (and probably other acts as well) is monetary compensation. The aborted fetus, according to the ruling, is not considered a human with the right to life. It is the loss to the woman and her husband that entails legal responsibility.

The case goes on, however, to rule on injury to the woman. She is legally enfranchised, so her injury or death is assessed according to the logic of equivalence (the *lex talionis*). I believe that the law-giver is simply affirming the general principle that the woman (but not the fetus) possesses the right to life and health, and violation of those is punishable by the logic applied to all cases involving humans. The actual wording is "life for life." Since, however, her death is accidental, there should be no criminal guilt assessed (according to 21:13). The concept of murder cannot be applied to this case if the law is consistent. On the other hand, the ruling in the case of a goring ox (21:29–30) excludes a monetary compensation for her death. This would leave only the option of making the fighter(s) liable to capital punishment but with the possibility of ransom.

Before we leave the subject of injury and death resulting from fighting let us consider a possibility not covered in the provisions. What would the classification have been if one fighter had killed the other by stone or fist? This event would not have the premeditation and intention of killing required of murder. The killer intended harm, not death. Would the case still fall under murder on the grounds that the killer should not have resorted to lethal force (especially if a stone was used)? Or could the defendant plead that since the killing was inadvertent that he should be allowed to be ransomed? Would it make any difference if the victim had also picked up a stone or used his fists against the killer?

Death and injury of slaves by their masters makes up a special set (21:20–21, 26–27). Apart from the ruling in Exod 21:32, slaves are accorded the rights of humans in the Book of the Covenant.[22] If a master assaulted his slave with a lethal weapon, it would, I am sure, be classified as a capital crime.[23] The complication arises when a master uses an instrument for beating (a "rod") and beats his slave to death (Exod 21:20–21). The law-giver assumes that the master has the right to beat his slave to force him or her to work. If the beating results in death, it is putatively accidental, for who would want to destroy his own investment? There is a distinction made, however: if the slave dies during or soon after the beating, the master should have known that he was exercising unwarranted force; hence, he becomes guilty of a felony ("punishable"), though of what class it does not say. If the slave survives a day or two, the court can assume that the master did not know how much harm he was inflicting at the time. The only punishment is extra-legal, his loss of his investment.

The right of beating is further circumscribed in 21:26–27. If a slave loses an eye or tooth as a result of the master's beating, he or she will be compensated by manumission. The slave, according to this ruling, is entitled to bodily integrity despite being owned by another. The master should know when his exercise of force is excessive.[24]

It should be clear form this tour of provisions that biblical law operates with the concept of causation and responsibility characteristic of any legal system worthy of the name. It is capable of being reconstructed by an interpreter who reasons from rulings to generalizations.

The Hierarchy of Being

If the biblical concept of causation and responsibility is rather standard, the metaphysical scheme embedded in its law is quite distinctive. To be sure, hierarchies of being are a common possession of the human mind. Each class of beings, according to it, has its own intrinsic qualities which determine its relationship of subordination or superordination to other classes. When a member of a class in one way or another transgresses the position of its class, a breach of the hierarchical order has occurred and must be repaired by some form of "composition." Biblical monotheism is distinct by its elevation of one deity, YHWH, to exclusive superiority,[25] and the human race, created in the image of God, above all other creatures.[26]

The goring ox is one of a very few cases which considers a breach by beings below humanity. The beast that kills a human has transgressed its subordination to the human race. This subordination is given its justification in the account of creation found in Genesis 1. Humanity is created "in the image of God" (Gen 1:26–27) and given "dominion over the fish of the sea . . . and over every living thing that moves upon the earth" (vv. 26, 28). Neither humans nor animals are supposed to kill and eat other creatures with "soul" (נֶפֶשׁ); they are to be satisfied with plants (which have life but not soul) for food (1:29–30). But alas, violence enters the created order and God, after the great flood, institutes an order allowing the eating of flesh (Gen 9:1–7). Humans are allowed to kill and eat any animal as long as the blood is drained. Animals are not explicitly granted permission to kill for food, but that seems to be understood. However, human beings are not to be killed for food or any other reason. "For your (human) lifeblood I (= God) will surely require a reckoning; of every beast I will require it and of a human . . ." (9:5). It is this injunction, protecting the metaphysical hierarchy, that the ox has violated. To restore the hierarchy, the offending animal must be destroyed.

The only other provision in the Book of the Covenant which may involve a beastly violation of the hierarchical order is sexual intercourse between humans and animals. "Whoever lies with a beast will be put to death" (Exod 22:18). Only the human party is concerned in this ruling. However, I suspect that the animal would be destroyed as well. The Holiness Code imposes the death penalty on both human and animal (Lev 20:15-16). It also suggests the classification of the act by calling it a "confusion" or "mixture" (תֶּבֶל) by which the parties incur "uncleanness" (Lev 18:23). Were the Israelite jurists inclined to spell out their reasoning more fully, they could have said that the hierarchical order has been violated by an interaction which belongs within a species; each party has crossed a "metaphysical" boundary into the other's class.

With the partial and ambiguous exception of slavery, biblical law does not recognize different "metaphysical" classes of human beings. This is not to say that there are no legally sanctioned social hierarchies. Social classes are not recognized, but roles in the family and civil community are. According to Exod 21:15-17, a son or daughter who assaults or curses (verbal assault) a parent is liable to the death penalty. Exod 22:27 forbids cursing God or a ruler of the people, an offense which seems to have carried the death penalty.[27] The severity of these provisions indicates that a rather major principle was involved.

The legal force of the metaphysical hierarchy is felt above all in the provisions protecting YHWH's exclusive claim to deity in Israel. In the Book of the Covenant, the prohibition against acknowledging any deity but YHWH is formulated as a remedial law as well (Exod 22:19). The principle informing it is not the protection of the metaphysical hierarchy in general, but of YHWH's claim to exhaust metaphysical supremacy and sovereign authority within Israel. One might say that the first commandment combines metaphysical hierarchy with hierarchy of authority.

Cultic law protects the metaphysical hierarchy in another way: It demands respect for the majesty and holiness of the deity. Within the decalogue, the sabbath commandment reflects this concern (Exod 20:8-11). Within the Book of the Covenant, it is found in a set of laws governing the construction and use of altars consecrated to YHWH (Exod 21:24- 26) and in various religious duties (22:28-30, 23:10-19). Far from being an extraneous subject within a civil code, the proper comportment of the people of Israel to the holy is a constituent feature of its identity as the holy people (22:30).

The hierarchical order plays a significant role in biblical anthropology. Humans have a place in the hierarchy of a being "a little lower than God (or the divine beings)" (Ps 8:5). Although the psalmist considers this a position of great honor, it is also a limit which the human race seeks to surmount. The early chapters of Genesis explore, in a narrative mode, this metaphysical rebellion. The serpent seeks to persuade the woman that the "knowledge of good and evil" is desirable because it will make her "like God" (Gen 3:5). He insinuates that God is withholding this good from humans to protect His supremacy. After the trial and sentencing of serpent, woman, and man, God decides that the human race must be expelled from the garden because "this human creature has become like one of us, knowing good and evil; and now, lest he put forth his hand and take also of the tree of life, and eat, and live forever . . ." (3:22). God appears to admit that the serpent was partially right, that humans have succeeded in breaking the bounds of their place in the hierarchical order and become god-like. The danger is that they will seek to take possession of another divine attribute, immortality. God must draw a line, or better, erect a barrier, between Creator and creature, so death becomes the comprehensive symbol of human creatureliness.

In Genesis 11, humans decide to escape the limits of their being by building a tower to heaven. God again sees this as a threat to the hierarchical order: "Behold, they are one people, and they have all one language; and this is only the beginning of what they will do; and nothing that they propose will be impossible for them" (Gen 11:6). The last clause echoes a theological prerogative mentioned frequently in Scripture.[28] Since the specific threat comes from the collective effort of the human race, its punishment is the shattering of human unity.

These passages are sufficient to show that the concept of metaphysical hierarchy is an essential component in the biblical anthropology. The law protects the order of being. Since the very reason for law is human sin (see Frymer-Kensky:147-55), and the desire to escape the limitations of humanity established by this order is the fundamental sin, the hierarchy of being is the deep background of all law.

The Unquantifiable Human

Let us return to the provisions governing an ox who gores a human to death. The penalty, you will remember, for the owner who knew his ox to be dangerous is extremely severe: He is liable in his own life (Exod 21:29). This penalty can only be explained by a principle of Israelite law to the effect that no monetary value can be assigned to a victim's life. Unlike his ancient Near Eastern counterparts, the biblical law-giver could not take recourse to a "reasonable" solution, *viz.*, either a fixed fine or negotiated payment to compensate the family of the victim. The negligent owner had to suffer a loss equal to the victim: "life for life."

The refusal to assign monetary value to human life runs through biblical law. Whenever we meet a case of felonious homicide, the law stipulates "life for life." If the killing is judged to be accidental, the killer does not suffer in his person, but he must accept temporary exile as a kind of metaphysical and social composition (Num 35:26-28, 32).[29] If the killing fell in the grey area (e.g., 2:20, 23, 22:2), we must assume something like the law of the goring ox, *viz.*, liability in one's life with the possibility of ransom.

The concept of ransom reinforces the principle of life for life. According to Num 35:31, ransom is specifically excluded for felonious homicide. The only value that a murderer can "give" equal to what he "took" is his or her own life.[30] To allow the murder to negotiate a monetary compensation would be seen as "buying off" justice. It would, of course, be an advantage to the rich and have the effect of differentiating the value of persons by class. The ox owner, however, has not willfully killed the victim of his ox, but acted negligently. His own death is not necessary to balance the ledger of justice. A negotiated payment is legally possible. However, the monetary sum is not assigned to the dead, but to the living. The logic of quantification is unique: How much is the owner willing to pay to save his life? One can guess that settlements were high.

In contrast to the "life for life" principle of crimes against persons, crimes against property are never punished by death, mutilation or, as far as the biblical texts themselves are concerned, physical punishment.[31] Whenever a remedy is mentioned, it is composition with compensation.[32] Humans and non-human property are incommensurable orders of being, and proportionate "repayment" must be in the same order of being as the crime (Finkelstein:36–39; see also Paul).

There is one case of theft that is punishable by death, the "stealing" of a human being (Exod 21:16). Kidnapping in ancient society was for the purpose of selling a person into slavery. A person who was captured would be sold to a trader who would transport the slave to a foreign country.[33] We can understand the law-giver's reasons for imposing capital punishment on the kidnapper: to rob a person of freedom and citizenship is a serious crime against the person, virtually equivalent to killing.[34]

The metaphysical hierarchy examined in the last section stands behind the unquantifiability of a human life. In particular, it is the concept that humans are created in the image of God that invests each life with incalculable value. According to biblical theology, the eternal Creator transcends the world of nature. It has a relationship to Him analogous to the relation of a pot to a potter (e.g., Isa 29:16). Humans are like all other creatures in this dependent status. However, God has endowed humans with the power of transcendence within creation. This not only bestows unique powers, it also bestows unique worth. Being in the image of God, each human is invested with God's incalculable value. Nothing in creation is of equal value save another human being; hence, the only "thing" a killer has equivalent to the life he or she took is his or her life. "Whoever sheds the blood of man, for (or by) man shall his blood be shed; for God made man in his own image" (Gen 9:6).

Gen 9:6 functions, if the ambiguous preposition, בְּ is to be translated "by," as an authorization of capital punishment. Capital punishment requires divine sanction, for humans cannot take life on their own authority; only the Creator who gives life has the authority to take it away. When they enforce God's sanctions against killers, they function as His representatives or agents.[35]

The Israelite court acts as God's agent in all of its judgments. The God of Israel is not only the authority behind the ultimate punishment, but all remedial actions. He is not only the Creator, but also the Redeemer who seeks to establish justice, righteousness, and loving-kindness in the life of His people. Whenever the court acts, it enforces these norms of communal life.

The God of Israel promises to supplement the action of His judicial representatives by direct intervention when there is no legal remedy or the legal remedy relies upon the moral earnestness of the society. In the Book of the Covenant, God promises to punish those who oppress the sojourner, widow, or orphan, or who make the debtor suffer (Exod 22:20-26). These divine sanctions are imposed according to the same standards of justice as the judicial system. When the cry of the victims rises to His ears, He will answer when the judges can or do not.

Unlike the human judicial system, however, God punishes "collectively." His punishment may extend beyond the culpable to later generations ("visiting the sins of the fathers upon the children and the children's children unto the third and fourth generations" [Exod 34:7]). Lurking behind this predication of God is a pervasive idea of biblical ethics: an evil deed has a way of setting a chain of events in motion which comes back to haunt either the perpetrator or his descendants (cp. Koch). Though this boomerang effect of evil deeds can be described as a veritable natural law, in Israelite monotheism it is subsumed under YHWH's exercise of authority as giver and enforcer of the law.[36]

Israelite law forbids collective punishment, at least collective capital punishment.[37] Deuteronomy expressly forbids putting parents to death for the acts of their children, or vice versa (24:17). It is this principle that explains the presence of the statement in the provisions for the goring ox: "If it gores a man's son or daughter, (the negligent owner) shall be dealt with according to the same rule" (Exod 21:31). The law-giver is excluding an overliteral application of the *lex talionis*, to the effect that "I lost my child, you must lose yours."

Why does God impose collective sanctions when He explicitly forbids Israelite judges to do so? It cannot be, as some argue, that He has privileged knowledge, because collective punishment is not based upon the idea that the "sons" of the culpable are themselves guilty. Indeed there appears to be no *legal* justification for collective divine punishment. The idea is more a matter of observation than legal theory. When breaches in the order of justice are not remedied, they fester. Law seeks to distribute justice precisely to avoid the indiscriminate justice of clan feuds, class vengeance, and the like. When legal remedies fail, collective justice comes into play.[38]

Jeremiah and Ezekiel address the discrepancy between the distributive justice of God's law and the collective justice imposed on His people. Their compatriots were complaining: "The fathers ate sour grapes and the children's teeth are set on edge" (Jer 31:29–30, Ezek 18:1–32). Both proclaim that this discrepancy will cease, that God will henceforth operate according to the principle of distributive justice. I count this a utopian, or perhaps eschatological, promise; history does not prove this tidy.

Conclusion

Does this study of biblical law as a humanities fit the bill? Does it offer a reading of the text which engenders understanding in the student? Will it interest students and give them pleasure? Will they have learned to think legally and to regard law as an exercise in public philosophy or theology?

I should hope that the answers are affirmative. It should be clear that law is much more than a technical practice, that it embodies concepts and principles of a "philosophical" order. Simply to understand the relatively obscure and marginal case of a goring ox, the interpreter must reconstruct the assumed concept of causation and responsibility, the assumed metaphysical hierarchy, and the system of value derived from that hierarchy's anthropology. When the scope of study expands to groups of provisions on related topics, one can discover an intricate, calibrated system of thought.

Of course, it is always possible to doubt this type of reconstruction. One can attribute the peculiar twists and turns of the provision on the goring ox to "primitive" ideas about responsibility and liability, and deny the intent of the framers of the lawbooks to have the provisions integrated by the interpreter. This reductionistic interpretive stance, however, violates the hermeneutical principle that the interpreter should construe a text as the best text it can be.

The exegetical procedure being proposed calls upon the interpreter to bring various statements of the Book of the Covenant into harmony and fill in the gaps. Although these interpretive moves are considered anathema to critical scholarship, they are the standard operating procedure of practitioners of the law. One can assume that the framer of a biblical lawbook wrote for such an audience. The Book of the Covenant expects its audience, for example, to construct a conceptual system of causation and responsibility from its provision.

This is not to say that the system of concepts and principles of the Book of the Covenant is without any discrepancies and tensions. The exception made of the slave gored to death is a rather disturbing example. This exception classifies the slave as property, not a person with unquantifiable value. This must be deemed a mistake on the part of the framer of the lawbook, for it does not cohere with his treatment of the slave elsewhere in the book. The mistake is understandable, for slavery was not really compatible with Israel's theology and anthropology (see Hanson:110–31). Despite that, it was an accepted institution in the society, so the law-giver attempted with varying success to reconceptualize it. The tension left by the Book of the Covenant was felt by the authors of the Deuteronomic and Holiness codes, each of which devised virtually utopian provisions to resolve the tension.

The existence of tensions like those surrounding slavery show the difficulty of doing "public philosophy." The attitudes and institutions of a society are not as malleable as the idealist would like. Any theological statement made in law will involve compromises with the rather intractable stuff of human nature. It is amazing that the Israelite law-givers were able to carry through their revolutionary program as completely as they did, given the intellectual horizons of ancient Near Eastern culture and the universal inclinations of the human heart.

The study of biblical law as a humanities loses the powerful directness which traditional Jews have experienced in their transactions with the sacred text. However, the search for the theology, metaphysics, social philosophy and ethics of biblical law need not—indeed, should not—be abstracted from the legal and philosophic questions all humans confront. We have here a subtle, compelling conceptual scheme which can hold its own against all rivals. Indeed, most Western legal traditions are as much descendants as rivals. The unique value of each human, essentially a discovery of biblical law-givers, continues to inform the legal systems in which we live (so Finkelstein). The study of biblical law forces the modern reader to consider the philosophic framework which best supports and sustains this compelling value.

NOTES

[1] Legal positivism is discussed by numerous scholars, and the writings of Bentham and Austin are readily available. One can read selections of their writings in Morris.

[2] Marxist thought, which has exercised a greater influence outside of legal philosophy than within, is discussed by many scholars; his chief work on law is untranslated: *Kritik der Hegelschen Rechtsphilosophie*. A handy summary of his views is found in Friedrich:143–53.

[3] I have in mind John B. Rawls, James Boyd White, and Ronald Dworkin. The last of these three is, to my mind, much the most powerful: see his *Taking Rights Seriously, A Matter of Principle,* and *Law's Empire.*

[4] An example of a legal and anthropological tradition which has its roots in the Bible is traced by Finkelstein:48–85.

[5] More than 200 of the 425 pages of the English Edition (Cleveland and New York: Meridian, 1957) of the *Prolegomena* are devoted to law.

[6] A. Alt's classic, "The Origins of Israelite Law," available in Alt:79–132, set the agenda for form criticism for more than a generation; his theses have been disputed, but his conception of form criticism was accepted on all sides.

[7] I say "defective" with such assurance on the basis of Dworkin's relentless and powerful assault on legal positivism (1977:14–45 and elsewhere), conventionalism and pragmatism (1986:114–75).

⁸ Other approaches have arrived at the same conclusions. The work of anthropologist Mary Douglas on the concept of cultic purity supports at least indirectly the assumption that ancient law was systematic and consistent; see Douglas.

⁹ To demonstrate his recommended approach, he worked through the law of homicide in biblical lawbooks, very much as I do in this essay.

¹⁰ Given scholars will, to be sure, be inclined to specific methodologies, from word studies to form criticism to structuralist anthropology. What I am suggesting is that the conceptual approach as a whole is not wedded to any specific one of these, and should not be.

¹¹ The term "casuistic law" is a form critical category introduced to the scholarly community by Alt:81–132. I suggested a subdivision of this category into "primary" and "remedial" (1973:180–84).

¹² The ANE examples do not mention the destruction of the animal, which means that whatever happened to it was of no legal consequence. Dehorning the ox would actually be sufficient to neutralize its lethal power.

¹³ Probably a better term would be "composition," an act by which the legal and metaphysical order is reestablished by an event proportional to the violation.

¹⁴ I should note that there are no sanctuary laws that require the execution of a person who has ventured into forbidden holy precincts; the Levitical guards should be able to prevent that from happening. We do have narratives, like Leviticus 10, of death for violation of holy space.

¹⁵ Our own practice may go either way, punishment for criminal negligence, or a civil suit.

¹⁶ The drafter of the laws of Eshnunna knew enough to cover both and put them together (#53 of ox, ##54–55 of humans). Their being together is one more indication of the different metaphysics of Mesopotamian culture.

¹⁷ Daube (86–87) offers some thoughts on what would have constituted proof in court that the ox was indeed the cause of death.

¹⁸ This doctrine was set forth in its classic form by G. E. Moore, *Principia Ethica*. It is standard fare in ethics textbooks, e.g., Frankena. For a powerful critique of the doctrine, see MacIntyre:54–57 and here and there throughout.

¹⁹ For some reason, the biblical passages defining the two categories are formulated in rather imagistic, melodramatic prose.

²⁰ The law of asylum stated in Num 35:31–33 presupposes that an accidental killer has incurred a kind of objective guilt which requires him to remain in "exile" in the city of asylum until the high priest's death expiates his sin. Neither the Book of the Covenant nor the lawbook of Deuteronomy speak of long term asylum, so without Numbers 35 we would have no evidence for this "impersonal" kind of guilt. Is the concept of asylum enunciated in Numbers 35 presupposed by the other texts or is it an invention of the Priestly law-giver? Greenberg (1959:125–32) defends the antiquity of Numbers 35, but must construe "high priest" to be the priest of the city of asylum, not Jerusalem. Since that identification is quite uncertain, we must leave the question open.

²¹ If one person attacked the other, and the victim resisted, we would not have a fight but a case of assault.

²² Exod 21:2–11 grants rights to men and women who enter into the condition of servitude. The absence of qualifying clauses distinguishing slaves in all laws but 21:32 indicates that the law-giver probably intends to cover them as well, though one could argue that 21:32 is the rule to be universalized.

²³ The fact that maltreatment of a female slave is sufficient to void bondage (Exod 21:10–11) strongly suggests that criminal assault be remedied with proportionate severity.

²⁴ Responsibility was a decisive factor in the classification of property loss as well. The very definition of theft is the willful appropriation of another's belongings. Our discussion of responsibility has gone on long enough, though, and it should be sufficient to establish the interpretive process by which one can recover the concept in biblical literature.

²⁵ There are no laws commanding respect for other supernatural beings; indeed, any respect to beings other than YHWH is expressly prohibited.

²⁶ The question of Israel's "uniqueness" is frequently debated by scholars; my assertion is based upon Finkelstein:7–14 and elsewhere, though I do not share in his Feuerbachian reductionism.

²⁷ That is certainly the way it was taken in 1 Kgs 21:8–10. In the case of God and rulers, it is respect due *authority* that has been violated by cursing.

²⁸ Cp. Gen 18:14, Job 42:2.

²⁹ See the paper by Peter Haas in this volume. Not only is this a metaphysical restoration, it is also a "cooling off" period for the family of the victim. It is uncertain whether this concept of asylum is presupposed by the earlier lawbooks or not.

³⁰ Daube:102–153 argues that the original meaning of "life for life" in the *lex talionis* was the replacement of the dead person provided by the killer. Though this is far-fetched, both substitution and monetary compensation for murder was in fact stipulated from time to time in ANE law, e.g., The Hittite Laws.

³¹ Scourging is treated in Deut 25:1–3, but we have no legal formulation stipulating this penalty.

³² Note the formula, שלם ישלם, to "complete," "restore," "repay."

³³ If an enslaved person remains in his or her own country, he or she could seek legal redress.

³⁴ One might also hear the repulsion of Israelite culture with the reduction of a human to monetary value.

³⁵ Since Gen 9:6 is addressed to Noah, the father of all races and nations, I construe it as an authorization of the law of homicide for all legal systems. A case can be made, however, for restricting it to Israel. Not all nations in fact impose the death penalty for murder, and few apply the other commandment given to Noah, *viz*, draining the blood of a slaughtered animal. My view is that the author (P) believes that all nations should comply with these rules, whether they in fact do so or not.

³⁶ There is another kind of collective punishment in biblical literature, the punishment of the community for the evil deeds of its members. This, I believe has a different logic than intergenerational punishment. The community must enforce the law through its leaders and the courts, and it incurs guilt when it fails its responsibility. Hence, the community does not really suffer for the deeds of its members, but for its own complicity in the violations and failure of will. I believe that the prospect of national guilt was first introduced into legal and covenant thinking by Deuteronomy; it may have been inchoate in earlier periods, but it was not embedded in the law and paranesis until Deuteronomy: see Patrick 1974:1–13.

³⁷ Most legal systems "punish" children economically for the "sins" of their parents, at least to the degree of sharing the common fate and under some circumstances of inheriting debt.

³⁸ It is because black slaves were not recognized as humans with full civil rights that our forefathers' sins were and still are visited on us centuries later.

WORKS CITED

Alt, Albrecht
    1966   *Essays on Old Testament History and Religion.* Oxford: Basil Blackwell.

Childs, Brevard
    1974   *The Book of Exodus.* Old Testament Library. Philadelphia: Westminster.

Daube, David
 1969 *Studies in Biblical Law.* New York: KTAV.

Douglas, Mary
 1966 *Purity and Danger.* London: Routledge and Kegan Paul.

Dworkin, Ronald
 1977 *Taking Rights Seriously.* Cambridge: Harvard University.
 1985 *A Matter of Principle.* Cambridge: Harvard University.
 1986 *Law's Empire.* Cambridge: Belknap-Harvard University.

Finkelstein, J. J.
 1981 *The Ox That Gored.* Transactions of the American Philosophical Society, 71, Pt. 2. Philadelphia: American Philosophical Society.

Frankena, William K.
 1963 *Ethics.* Englewood Cliffs, NJ: Prentice-Hall.

Friedrich, Carl Joachim
 1963 *The Philosophy of Law in Historical Perspective.* 2d ed. Chicago: University of Chicago.

Frymer-Kensky, Tikva
 1977 "The Atrahasis Epic and Its Significance for Our Understanding of Genesis 1–9." *BA* 40:147–55.

Greenberg, Moshe
 1959 "The Biblical Conception of Asylum." *JBL* 78:125–32.
 1960 "Some Postulates of Biblical Criminal Law." *Yehezkel Kaufmann Jubilee Volume.* Ed. M. Haran. Jerusalem: Magnes Press.

Hanson, Paul
 1977 "The Theological Significance of Contradiction within the Book of the Covenant." Pp. 110–31 in *Canon and Authority: Essays in Old Testament Religion and Theology.* Ed. George Coats and Burke Long. Philadelphia: Fortress.

Koch, Klaus
 1955 "Gibt es ein Vergeltungsdogma im A.T.?" *ZTK* 52:1–42.

MacIntyre, Alasdair
 1981 *After Virtue.* Notre Dame: University of Notre Dame.

Maine, Henry Sumner
 1861 *Ancient Law: Its Connection with the Early History of Society and its Relation to Modern Ideas.* Boston: Beacon. Reprinted, 1963.

Moore, G. F.
 1954 *Judaism in the First Centuries of the Christian Era.* Vol. I. Cambridge: Harvard University.

Morris, Clarence
 1959 *The Great Legal Philosophies.* Philadelphia: University of Pennsylvania.

Paul, Shalom M.
 1970 *Studies in the Book of the Covenant in the Light of Cuneiform and Biblical Law.* VTSup 18. Leiden: Brill.

Patrick, Dale
 1973 "Casuistic Law Governing Primary Rights and Duties," *JBL* 92:180–84.
 1974 "Collective Address in Deuteronomic Law." *American Academy of Religion: Biblical Literature, 1974:*1–13.
 1985 *Old Testament Law: An Introduction.* Atlanta: John Knox.

LOGIC AND ISRAELITE LAW

Martin J. Buss
Emory University

ABSTRACT

An examination of the logical structure of Israelite law can make use of deontic logic (dealing with norms) as well as of intensional logic (dealing with beliefs, etc.). The following basic elements play key roles in a model that fits biblical data closely: (1) a fundamental relational-objective reality, with room for both particularity and generality; (2) norm and evaluation as correlative elements; (3) kinds of action; (4) rightness as a standard for valuable action, with a connotation of privilege; (5) consequence; (6) contribution as an enhancing action, associated with a value judgment; (7) decreasing, or destructive, activity as a problem and as a response.

It is easy to see that legal statements have a practical aspect. Laws, however, also have an intellectual side. It is the aim of the present essay—as of others in the current issue of *Semeia*—to focus on this latter dimension. The study will do so by availing itself of the aid provided by deontic logic, that is, the logic of norms. Its purpose is not so much to provide new exegetical details as to show the theoretical aspect of legal provisions.[1] The term "Israelite law," incidentally, will be taken quite broadly to refer to expressly stated norms of the Hebrew Bible.

Symbolic Logic

As is true for most of modern logic, deontic logic employs symbols which abbreviate categories or elements which enter into the logic. In other words, it is a symbolic logic. Many different systems have been developed. Indeed, it is commonplace in modern logic not to recognize any one true set of principles, but to show the consequences of different assumptions or procedures. For instance, one might show what can consistently happen (intellectually) if one does not assume that statements are always either true or false but allows them to have an intermediate (indeterminate) truth value.

The use of symbols has been found to be extremely helpful, since they increase one's ability to check the tightness of logical conclusions and provide a stimulus for exposing hidden assumptions. Resulting reflections often lead to the correction of an analysis and to further developments of it.

Thus it is interesting to watch how, in the history of deontic logic, proposals made have been modified as problems emerged in regard to them. The present paper has undergone several revisions, as the use of symbolism exposed ambiguities that are easily hidden by informal modes of expression.

A system of notation is, of course, meaningless, if the symbols are not interpreted. Commonly, a meaning is given by stating a theorem or proposition in ordinary language, intuitively (without formal precision, but as consistently as possible). Indeed, the majority of the present essay will be expressed in ordinary English. Formal notation will be used only intermittently as a kind of check on what is being said. One can argue that in normal scholarly writing the use of logical symbols should be avoided altogether (or confined to footnotes), even when one's thinking has been aided by the use of such symbols; the present essay, however, is intended to draw explicit attention to the intellectual process.

There are a number of deontic systems that are currently recognized as coherent options.[2] It is not necessary to adjudicate between such alternatives because of the open-ended nature of logic just indicated. Many issues in deontic—and more specifically in juristic—logic, however, remain inadequately explored. If the present paper makes a contribution to professional philosophy, it will be in the form of posing problems that require closer attention.

In fact, no full-fledged deontic logic or complete formalization of biblical law or ethics is attempted here; only fragments of a formal logic are presented. Primary emphasis is placed on the semantic aspect of such a logic (as developed since the 1950s in close conjunction with model theory), with a focus on the structure or potential meaning of individual propositions. The chain of reasoning that can lead from one proposition to another is indicated informally. At the end of the paper appear a few hints about the larger context of the specific analyses.

We shall begin by furnishing a classification of the symbols to be used— in other words, by describing their syntax. One set of symbols will be lowercase letters in Roman print. They will stand for particulars, which need not be actual. Among these, the letters p and q will stand for particular situations expressible by combinations of two or more other signs; the letters x and y will be variables in formulas with a quantifier "all" or "some." A second group of symbols are capital letters, which will designate general categories, which are applicable to more than one (actual or hypothetical) object or situation. Such categories include predicates (red, tall, etc.) and modalities (e.g., possible, right).[3] A third group of symbols includes nonletter signs for such sentence operators as negation (~) and for two basic kinds of relations, namely perspective (:) and consequence (>), to be discussed below. Parentheses will be used to express "all" (or "any") and to group other symbols when it is necessary to do so to avoid confusion.

This classification implies, for the present writer—as well as for the biblical thought to be represented—an ontological assumption, namely, that reality includes both particulars and general categories. Neither of these two aspects is, in such a view, reducible to the other; rather, both are regarded as reflecting a relational structure, which exhibits an ultimate reality (to be discussed later).

Deontic Logic and Language About God

Deontic symbols express a special kind of modality. We shall use R for "it is right" and O for "it ought to be." Their meanings and mutual relations will be examined further, below.

Rightness or oughtness can be understood as actually or potentially related to a normative system, which may or may not be embodied in the outlook or will of an individual. One can thus write as follows: a:Op ("according to a, it ought to be that p"). A statement of the form a:Op is externally descriptive; it asserts that a certain reality requires, wills, or desires something. If the initial cluster (a:) is omitted, so that only Op remains, the resulting statement is an "internal" expression[4] of a command, etc—either one's own or that of someone else whom one seeks to represent. Similarly, Tp, "p is true [in actuality]," is the internal version of a:Tp, "according to a, p is true" or "a believes that p."

The fact that a:Op describes a desire or will has led to the thesis that a statement of the form Op is "emotive," expressing an emotion or volition. This thesis is true; but the opinion, often joined with it, that emotive expressions are arbitrary does not follow from it, any more than one needs to assume that statements expressing a belief are taken out of thin air.

One can discuss the issue in terms of recent analyses of possible worlds (or models). Possible worlds are systems of hypothetical states; insofar as they are related to human life, possibilities represent the content of thought and imagination.[5] Included among possible worlds are those which are to a greater or lesser extent ideal; an imperative or wish refers to such an ideal world.

Some philosophers argue for objectivity in regard to actuality (holding that the actual exists without reference to an observer) but reject objectivity in regard to the ideal. Yet, it is quite likely that neither the actual nor the ideal is independent of interaction,[6] and one may hold that not only beliefs, but also ideals, can be valid (or invalid) according to standards that are not solipsistic. Furthermore, it seems that practical reason—the reason involved in praxis, which includes ideality—is fundamental in relation to empirical description so that the validity of the latter (description) must be based on a validity of the former (praxis).

Biblical literature has answered the question of objectivity (rightly or wrongly) by referring to an ultimate perspective, that of God, both in regard to truth and in regard to value. If one likes—but this is only one possibility for a conceptualization—one can understand God's perspective as one which an intersubjective view approaches as it increases in comprehensiveness and sensitivity.[7]

How is God to be symbolized? Often God is treated as a particular entity. It is probably best, however, to treat God as a not-fully-graspable reality which includes both particularity and generality, to be modeled by a relational structure, which, taken as primitive, implies both dimensions.[8] In the Hebrew Bible, the particular and general aspects of the divine are expressed, at least roughly, by the use of the name Yahweh for the former and of the abatract plural Elohim for the latter. This distinction in usage, to be sure, is not rigid; but the commands to Adam, Eve, and Noah, representing all of humanity, are promulgated by Elohim (Gen 1:28; 9:1–7) while the laws directed to Israel through Moses are given by Yahweh. In order to avoid treating divine reality simply as a particular or simply as a universal, a star (*) will be used for it. For biblical literature, Op then is expressed by *:Op ("according to God, p ought to be" or "God wills that p").

This formulation takes account of two potentially diverging considerations. On the one hand, there is good reason to hold that norms somehow stand in a relationship to the attitudes of persons (or sentient beings), although the precise nature of this relation is debated. On the other hand, a norm must be general if it is not to be a free creation by each individual, which in practice means either a chaotic free-for-all or the victory by force of some arbitrary will. Indeed, a norm can be inwardly affirmed by an individual as binding (and not just tolerated as an imposed force) only if it is viewed as intersubjective in character—expressing neither simply one's own, nor simply another's, will—such as one symbolized by *:Op.

There is a religious tradition which views ethical norms as due to the free decision of God; this tradition regards God primarily as a particular, so that any general structure is secondary. It has found important representatives within Christianity since the latter part of the Middle Ages.[9] Although it is true that very little in biblical literature addresses this issue, some texts point in the opposite direction. According to Genesis 1, God "sees" that the reality created by the divine word is "good." If God were an arbitrary creator of the standards of goodness, such a statement would be pointless; one might instead expect a statement that God called the order good. According to Deut 4:6, other nations will come to admire how "wise" is Israel for having such laws. Thus, in representing biblical thought there is no justification for treating divine laws as rooted in a purely particular will.

Before proceeding to a discussion of imperatives in the Bible, it is well to look first at the relation between imperatives and wishes, on the one hand, and evaluations, on the other. The contrast between these two major subdivisions of valuational language is well illustrated by Genesis 1. A sentence of the former kind (which may use the word "ought") logically precedes an action or event. Thus in the creation story the statement "Let there be light," precedes and brings about the existence of light. An evaluation—which can be expressed by saying that something is "good" or "bad"—inherently succeeds an action or event.[10] One can symbolize a positive evaluation of a particular event or action by Gp, "it is good that p." (A full analysis needs to specify for whom, or for what, it is good and to state, or imply, a perspective; e.g. $a{:}G_bp$, "a believes that p is good for b.")

Within the structure of biblical speech as a whole, one sees a similar duality in the relation of the predominant emphasis of the Pentateuch to that of the Prophets. The Pentateuch contains numerous inculcations, presenting a normative pattern for action. Prophetic speech involves, in part, a reaction to events, with an evaluation. This duality shows how biblical literature can be understood in terms of a pragmatic-valuational structure and its logic.

Preceptive Stipulations

The inculcations of the Torah contain several types. One type directly states norms in the second or third person, rather than implying them by announcing a penalty. This type is often called "apodictic," but may more clearly be called "preceptive," since it does not include the curses and announcements of the death penalty which A. Alt included under the former heading. Symbolization for this kind can be thus: $(x)(RFx)$, "for all x, it is right that x have the characteristic F." The characteristic F usually refers to involvement in an activity of a certain kind.[11]

One feature of these laws should be noted explicitly, namely that they refer to types of actions and not to particular acts. This is not surprising and, indeed, is true for anything that is normally called "law." Yet it calls for comment. It assumes that one can meaningfully speak of types or kinds of realities. Modern ethics has attempted to create alternate approaches that attribute rightness or wrongness to particular actions rather than to types of them, in line with a strongly particularist orientation in modern philosophy. A major branch of utilitarianism is a representative of such an approach to ethics. The theologies of Brunner (70) and Barth (740) had a particularist thrust in holding that God has a command for each occasion. Such particularism, however, is plainly out of step with the orientation of the Hebrew Bible.

In positive formulations employing the Hebrew imperfect, "may" and "shall" are not distinguished; only the context can determine which of these meanings is intended. For instance, translators regularly use "may" in Lev 11:2, 3, 9, 21 (for permitted foods); 21:3 (permitted defilement); and Deut 23:20 (taking interest from a foreigner). Thus in representing Hebrew laws, one may want to employ the cautious symbol R ("it is right") instead of the stronger O ("it ought to be"); R is the broader term, which includes O as a subdivision. O can be defined in terms of R thus: $Op = {\sim}R{\sim}p$ ("it is not right that not p"); then O~p is equivalent to ~Rp ("it is not right that p"). In an "open" legal system, in which not all actions are regulated, it is appropriate to apply three-valued logic to R, so that (~R)p for a rejected action is distinguished from ~(Rp) for an action for which there is no express authorization or legitimation.[12]

To begin with R ("right") as a basic symbol is of considerable importance, for many of the biblical precepts, especially the positive ones, appear to embody privilege. Furthermore, it coheres well with what may be a psychological dynamic entering into ethics, namely that human beings, for effective action, need to be able to approve—i.e., affirm as a valuable option—that in which they are engaged.[13]

The notion of privilege or valuable action is most obviously applicable to cultic regulations, in which procedures are set forth for the accomplishment of weal; for, in the ancient world, sacrifices and other rituals were considered not so much duties as powerful means for good. A major cultic concern is whether deity is willing to receive an offering. Accordingly, the directions of Lev 1:3 (etc.) specify procedures for a ritual that will be "accepted." In a certain sense, a prophet can be justified, within a biblical framework, in saying that God has "not commanded" sacrifices (Jer 7:22); he can announce, indeed, that God will not accept them (Amos 5:22; Hos 18:13; Jer 14:10. 12; Mal 1:10, 13).

How far can one take such an interpretation of precepts as expressing privileges? Certainly, a number of the precepts (e.g., "keep the sabbath day holy") are joined with negative statements (such as, "you may not do any work" on that day) which make it clear that there is more than a permission at work; in fact, the Hebrew of this precept does not use the imperfect form, which, as noted, can state a permission. Nevertheless, there is a sense of joy which appears repeatedly in regard to keeping the precepts, so that the connotation of privilege is not inappropriate, at least as an overtone, also for those inculcations which clearly express requirements.[14] A number of precepts refer to beneficial consequences (e.g., long life for honoring one's parents, Exod 20:12); this fact contributes a positive flavor.

Sanctions for Precepts

The role of sanctions represents a central issue in deontic logic. Although precepts often do not refer directly to sanctions, both positive and negative results are announced in biblical literature at the conclusion of a legal complex within which precepts play a major role (such as Deuteronomy). One might say that rightful or wrongful behavior has consequences for the society. For instance, altruistic behavior, enjoined in a number of the precepts, normally benefits the community, even though not necessarily the ones who engage in it. An absence of individual rewards became a problem for wisdom, as is well known.

Naturally, it is of advantage to members of a community to apply informal pressure on their fellows to adhere to rightful actions, for instance, through praise or criticism. A belief in divine rewards or judgments can provide further support. In Israel, prophets appear to have had a role in expressing criticism, together with divine threats, especially in regard to the community as a whole or to its leaders.

How should divine sanctions be understood? One may regard them simply as the consequence of wishful thinking or as a cultural device to encourage socially beneficial (and discourage contrary) behavior. God would then be a more or less useful fiction. But what if consequences are rooted in the very nature of community life, which is an integral part of the cosmos? Perhaps the English "God" (and our *) can then be taken as a cipher for an ultimate dynamic order.[15] For a believer in such an order, the "is" and the "ought" (the actual and the ideal) need not be completely separate, although they are not identical or strictly derivable one from the other. In any case, in biblical thought morality is not valued simply for its own sake apart from consequences for oneself and others.

To represent consequence, we need a new symbol, as follows: $>$. Attempts to clarify the notion of consequence, in fact, lie behind much of modern modal logic (dealing with "possibility," etc.), of which deontic logic can be considered an extension. It appears that the notion of consequence must be a relatively basic one in logic, for it has not been possible to reduce it to other categories.[16]

For some deontic theories, the formula $p > s$, "a certain situation leads to a sanction," or a similar one, serves as a definition for $O\sim p$, "p ought not to be"; a sanction, in such a formula, is usually characterized as something "bad" for the person to whom it is applied. Such a theory treats the "good" as a more fundamental category than the "right," since the latter is understood in terms of the former. A sanction, however, is specifically a legal consequence, so that the notion of the "right" is already contained within it.[17] Thus we will treat the presence of a sanction not as a part of the definition of the right, but as a separately statable characteristic.[18] The absence of strict individual retribution for preceptively worded norms reflects this looseness of connection.

Penal and Remedial Law

The notion of consequence is, however, integral to law that is either penal or remedial in character. This realm—law in a narrow sense, as distinguished from ethics or cult—can be subdivided, at least roughly, into criminal and civil law.[19] The peculiar structures of these different kinds of stipulation are shown conveniently by means of symbolism.

Criminal law may be defined as law that deals with conflicts between an individual and a community which exercises penal authority and power over that individual. These are not merely cases of strife between members of the group, which are handled by civil law. In relatively mild cases, the penalty can be that of beating (e.g., Deut 25:2). In more serious situations, the community can protect itself from an aggressor against it, and discourage future conflicts, by removing the offender from the society (cf. Black:127) by expulsion, death, or imprisonment. Imprisonment, the favored modern response, was rarely used in Israel (and elsewhere in the ancient world) as a penal process. Instead, death was the favored official penalty, although this was often modified in practice.

The death penalty can be stated as follows: $(x)(Fx > RK'x)$, "for any x, if x engages in F, it is right that x is killed." The Hebrew of this is often translated by saying that such and such a person "shall surely be put to death." The idiom employed, however, does not express certainty but draws special attention to the situation indicated by the verb;[20] in legal texts (including those of civil law), it states a liability.

Who determines and carries out the death penalty? In most of the Israelite criminal laws, the penalty is authorized by the community or by its head and carried out either by the authorities themselves (e.g., by the assemblage through stoning) or by a representative. One can write: $(x)(Fx > RcKx)$, "... it is right that the community kills x." There are some laws in which the right to put to death may be spread rather widely. One set of these occurs in relation to major cases of incest and for bestiality. For these it is stated that the offenders' "blood is upon them" (Lev 20:11, 12, 16). That quite possibly means that no blood guilt occurs when they are killed; in other words, anyone may put them to death, as is expressed by the following formulation: $(x)(y)(Ix > RyKx)$, "for any x and any y, if x commits a major case of incest, it is right for y to kill x."[21]

There are indeed various indications that the execution of the death penalty was conceived of as a right (i.e., as legitimate[22]) and not necsssarily as a duty. These indications appear both in biblical stories and in rabbinic discussions which place precautionary restraints upon the death penalty and on flogging.[23] In practice, expulsion or exile to a designated location was probably a common result of a major transgression. For modern law, it has been similarly argued that penalties are a right, not a duty, of the community (so, Raz:84-86, following H. Kelsen). In both ancient and modern societies, actual penalties are adjusted to fit the overall circumstances.

It should be noted that a criminal law has two sides. On the one hand, it is oriented toward a potential violator. In that direction, it acts as a deterrent by indicating what may happen as a result of a certain deed, so that then we have a predictive "may"; what will actually occur depends, of course on a number of factors, including whether the act will be discovered. On the other hand, the law is oriented toward the community which is faced with the problem action. In this regard, the community has the right (a permissive "may") and, to some extent at least, a duty to keep itself in proper shape.[24]

Civil law, as already stated, deals with conflicts or problem situations within a community. Two litigants may bring a question before a judge for adjudication.

Very widespread in the Near East—perhaps also in Israel—was the view that a judge's verdict was not in itself binding, but had to be accepted by the litigants; going to a series of judges was a possibility.[25] It is known that Mesopotamian settlements commonly do not invoke legal statutes in their support. Thus there is ground to believe that the provisions stated in Israelite civil law—for instance, those of *lex talionis*—were not strictly obligatory.[26] Undoubtedly, however, they should be thought of as more than mildly recommended.

The provisions of civil law do not mention penalties for the failure of a defendant to carry out the stipulated remedy. This fact reflects an assumption of noncriminal processes that the defendant is not fundamentally hostile to the community but will cooperate with a reasonable judgment, especially if it is supported by social pressure, and may, in fact, want to do what is right.

An important subcategory of civil law is that of torts, involving compensation for injury or damage. A typical case of this sort can be formulated thus: $(x)(y)(xDy > RxCy)$, "for any x and y, x's acting to the detriment of y leads to its being right that x contributes to y." In this statement, D is interpreted as meaning "being responsible for a decrease of, or detriment to," someone; a significant element in this definition is that of responsible action, which can be less or more than what a person's body effects.[27] C represents a corresponding positive action.

Although the difference between the formula for torts and the one for criminal cases reflects a basic difference between these two main types of law, the two structures can be assimilated to some extent. Often, x's contributing to y will mean a certain decrease for x. Instead of $RxCy$, "it is right that x contributes to y" (part of the tort formula), one might then say that $RyDx$, "it is right that y decrease (take from) x." Such a right—only partially stated in the Bible[28]—is based on another person's obligation. Insofar as this interpretation is admissible it is true that in both kinds of situations the injured party (the private individual or the community) has the right to protect its interest through an action which is to the detriment of the one who has brought about the injury. This might be stated as an axiom, as follows: $(x)(y)(xDy > RyDx)$.

Concluding Remarks

In reflecting upon the structure within which specific Israelite legal and ethical stipulations are placed, one can observe that penal and remedial provisions are basically negative in character, furnishing rightful responses to problems. They can do no more than redress or forestall evil and do not by themselves support the increase of the good. A society also requires positive inculcations and such as have no stated penalties, some of which have the simple form RxCy, "it is right that x contribute to y." These play a significant role within precepts (e.g., "love the stranger," Deut 10:19).

The patterns noted are hardly peculiar to Israel, although certain features may well be emphasized in biblical literature more than elsewhere. It is indeed likely that the fundamental logical pattern of biblical law is continuous with that of law (and ethics) generally. If that is the case, support is given to the view that law is more than an arbitrary creation of an individual or of a group.

In biblical literature, a basis for both the positive and the negative structures lies in God's creation of Israel (in the Exodus, etc.) and of the rest of the world. One can write (with subscripted p for the past tense): $(x)(*C_p y)$, "for all x, God has contributed to (created) y." Part of the definition of C, as given above, is that a responsible action is involved. If responsibility includes conscious intention and if the agent acts in a rationally moral manner, xCy implies x:RC'y, "according to x, it is right that y receives a contribution." Specifically, God's creating y means that, according to God (a fundamentally and universally true perspective), it is right that y is given being. A contribution to y by a human being, together with its associated value judgment, is then in line with a divine (truly valid) perspective and action.[29]

Divine creation, however, is pictured in Israel (and elsewhere) as allowing for, and (one may say) supporting divergence, which gives rise to tension and conflict. When conflict leads to a decrease for a being within God's care, remedial action is called for. In fact, penal action diminishing or eliminating a destructive actor is permitted and may be required. Thus there is a legitimate role for negative effects.

To state more precisely the relation between such categories as being (or richness of existence), contribution, and decrease is a task that goes beyond the limit of the present paper. It involves questions of organization and growth. For instance, it is well established that negative feedback, of which pain can be a form, is preservative and that positive feedback, including pleasure, leads to change or development. It may be that fullness of being should be taken as a fundamental value (as can be appropriate to an ethic based on rightness[30]).

Further analysis will probably also be able to relate to divine care much of the content of Israelite law, such as a concern for the weak. In doing so, it may reveal a grounding for intermediate postulates that may be set forth.

Perhaps the analyses that have been made show that in theology—as in more partial visions—reflective principles are operative, with an observable coherence. It is likely that biblical studies, in examining sacred texts, can contribute to the apprehension of faith by laying bare the logical structure of what is said. As has been observed, the applicable logic needs to be dynamic, one that deals with such concepts as "action" and incorporates value-laden terms like "right."

NOTES

[1] For a defense of the view that laws have a logic, see Weinberger and, in part, Falk:152–91. If the logic applied is a valuational one, as will be argued, there is no inherent conflict between a logical and a dynamic approach.

[2] For overviews of the history of deontic logic and presentations of more or less viable options, see, e.g., Kalinowski; von Wright:1981; Chellas; and Aqvist.

[3] Predicates and modalities may be distinguished roughly on pragmatic grounds, but they seem to belong together for logical theory. One can understand modalities, as well as predicates, as actual or potential relations (similarly, Lewis:187, 189; Bond:96); thus it is not necessary to choose between a "relational" and a "modal" view of intensions, such as beliefs. (Castañeda:335 draws together these two views, without altogether identifying them.)

[4] So also Wedberg:258.

[5] A conceptualist (moderately nominalist) view considers possibilities as dependent on thought; a more or less moderate realist can regard possibilities as having a degree of reality of their own but may define thought as that which deals with possibilities.

[6] Apparently, even on the physical level, entities are not determinate without interaction with another one. Ideals may not be independent of what is called "God."

[7] Such an understanding is comparable to Peirce's standard for truth, except that Peirce seems to have understood the comprehensive view as one toward which science tends in actuality (7.78). An intersubjective view as an ideal perspective—combining relationality with a kind of objectivity—appears also in Putnam:216 (for truth) and Nagel:130 (for ethics—Nagel:64 appropriately connects this duality with the self-transcendence which is involved in self-awareness, arising in a social process). One can, even more fundamentally, speak of God as lying at the heart of the communicative structure itself (as mentioned by Habermas:121), identifiable with love. The conceptions of a basic communicative structure and of a comprehensive perspective are united in the idea of unlimited communication (which runs from Peirce, via H. G. Mead and K. Jaspers, to several recent thinkers, including Habermas).

[8] That a relation implies particularity as well as generality has effectively been argued by Bertrand Russell; further, he viewed these two dimensions as inherent aspects of propositions (199), which, of course, represent a basic element of communication.

[9] Such a view appears already in "orthodox" Islam, which may have influenced Christian positions, formulated in conjunction with a rising individualism. In Muslim theory, however, the theoretical statement that morality is based on God's free decision is joined with a thesis affirming the eternal existence of the Koran, so that the will revealed there is not, really, secondary; this dual view looks like an inconsistency, but reflects what can be judged to be a sound intuition. A believer (of any tradition) who grounds divine authorship of the moral order in the qualities of God (Reeder:36) is not a particularist.

[10] No claim is made that "ought" and "good" always have the meanings here discussed. In terms of the definitions employed, "ought" can be used for a past event when that is set in relation to a past frame work (e.g., "yesterday [it was true that] he ought to have done thus") and "good" can refer to a future evaluation ("it will be good that ..."). In any case, deontic logic needs to be merged with temporal logic. The relative temporal relation of "ought" and "good" in regard to an actual or hypothetical event does not necessarily represent the ultimate theoretical order of the categories mentioned, for it is possible that an imperative or wish is based on an anticipation of good, which itself may be based on a past experience of value. The question will here be left open; "right" and "good" will simply be regarded as correlated.

[11] One can make explicit that certain restrictions are placed upon the nature of x (e.g., that it be human or Israelite), but we will omit these qualifications for simplicity's sake. Quite a few precepts specify certain conditions, expressed with a "when"; they shade over into but can be distinguished from, those "when you" stipulations referred to in note 24, below.

[12] In a two-valued (closed) legal system, it makes no difference whether one starts with R (the expressly permitted) or with O (obligation); in a three-valued system, some difference does result (see Philipps). Legitimacy or rightness has been taken as a basic symbol for deontic logic by Garcia Maynez (18), von Wright (in Davis:105), and Lampe (41); similarly. also by Griffin:331, 333. Reliance on the notion of the "right" reduces, although it does not completely eliminate, the problem of a conflict between norms, which easily arises with strict "oughts."

[13] Somewhat similarly, Gewirth:48–52. This dynamic is an important part of culture, comparable to, but different from, social behavior based on instinct.

[14] E.g., Ps 119:14, 16, 20, etc. For rabbinic joy in the law, see Schechter:147–69. According to the thirteenth-century Ha-Hinnuk, the commandments reflect (only) God's desire "to do good to us" (Appel:83).

[15] I. Kant (224) rightly noted that a harmony between ideality and reality is expressed by a belief in God. The relation of morality to views of the world in religious systems is also noted by Donagan:28.

[16] For the symbol > and an acute discussion of its logic, see Stalnaker and Thomason. In the present study, a symbolism for either "material" or "formal" implication or for "relevance logic" is avoided; "if" or "when," as used here, refers to the antecedent of >.

[17] So, rightly, e.g., O. Weinberger in Lenk:110, rejecting sanction-based views of obligation as developed by several deontic logicians as well as by some theorists of law (in this, Weinberger is in line with such notable theorists as John Austin and H. L. A. Hart). The sanction formula, however, has been given a broader interpretation by the early proponent A. Anderson, so that it does not necessarily involve punishments and no longer implies a reduction of norms to another level (in Davis:110; similarly, already, A. Prior in Meldon:146 and S. Kanger in Hilpinen:36–58). Penalties (other than natural consequences) reflect the superior strength of an authority (von Wright, 1963:128) and, thus, are partly nonrational. Berman (28) argues—perhaps correctly—that, psychologically, coercion is not the fundamental basis for obedience to law; according to Erikson (222), a relatively mature ethics involves "a ready consent to a formulated good," without necessary reference to penalties. A theory of law based on consequences would give priority to the "good" over the "right."

[18] The need for a sanction can be based on the principle that someone who wills something also wills at least some means to its end. Thus an authority giving a command naturally employs, at least implicitly, motivating sanctions.

[19] Buss:1977, stimulated by H. Cazelles, discussed this distinction, together with instances of overlap. (See now, somewhat similarly, Greengus.) Cazelles had pointed out that third-person casuistic formulations in the Hebrew Bible represented, for the most part, what in the modern Continental tradition would be called "private law" (roughly, that in which a private party sues another and in which whatever payment is made as a settlement goes to the plaintiff). What is called "civil law" in the U.S. forms an even closer parallel, since this, like Israelite tort law, includes penal elements, with the penalties accruing as a "windfall" to the plaintiff. (E.g., according to Exod 21:37, the plaintiff gets five oxen for the one stolen; similarly, in the U.S. a plaintiff can receive "punitive" payments beyond the actual loss.) The similarity between the U.S. and Israelite systems is probably due to their continuing an old tradition, which was revised in Roman law.

[20] Besides Bergstrasser (Buss, 1977:56), see now also Muraoka:83–92 (although the latter, in what appears to be an inconsistency, continues to speak of "absolute obligation"). An appropriate English translation can be: "... may be *killed* [with an emphasis on this word]" or, in writing "... may indeed be killed." (Such a threat is serious enough; whether, or to what extent, it is still legitimate in modern society must be left open, but the function of the ancient formula—protecting the integrity of a group—is, in any case, still relevant. For a discussion of the current issue and a criticism of the writer's view, see Bailey.)

[21] For the meaning of the formulation involved and comparative legal phenomena, see Buss, 1977:57–58 (with notes 27 and 28), extending an analysis by K. Koch (who has argued that an

absence of blood guilt is indicated but thinks that the reference is to an officially sanctioned executioner) and leaving open the possibility that expulsion from a divinely protected sphere is what is indicated (these two interpretations may have been closely connected in the ancient view).

[22] It should be clear that "right" here is not taken as based on an obligation placed upon some one else, but as a fundamental concept, related to reflective or critical willing. A right, however, may imply an obligation as a second step; for arguments regarding a priority of right over duty in faith—contrary to the idea of some—cf. Falk:77–81.

[23] See Gen 2:17 (cf. Buss, 1977:56, note 21); II Sam 14 (on Absalom). Rabbinic caution toward the death penalty ia well known; beatings, too, were subject to restriction (not only to the number thirty-nine, but also to a lesser number, if the condition of the offender justifies that [Makkot, 3]). It probably never occurred to the rabbis, and should not have, that they might be violating a divine command in exercising such restraints.

[24] The two sides are to some extent correlated with linguistic formulations. Participial and relative forms tend to act as deterring threats. The formulation in which the problem actor is given in the third person and the responding agent in the second (e.g., Exod 21:14; Deut 13:2–6; cf. Buss. 1977:59) is oriented more toward the community's response, although the purpose of this response is, in turn, clearly stated as that of being a deterrent (Deut 13:12; 17:13; 19:20; 21:21). Formulations like "you shall/may remove the evil from the midst of you" (Deut 13:6, etc.) have overtones of both obligation and right; cf. Deut 21:9, which is best read: "Thus you can remove innocent blood [guilt] from the midst of you, when you do what is right in the sight of Yahweh." After all, it is of advantage to the community to remove evil and guilt (cf. D. Wright.403), as stated in Deut 19:13. A relatively pure expression of duty to apply the death penalty appears in Exod 22:17: "You may not keep a sorceress alive."

[25] For some relevant data, see Buss, 1977:52 (with references in note 3); also Black:128–129; Wilson:235–36. It appears that ancient Near Eastern judicial solutions (especially for civil cases), like many elsewhere, had the status of proposals rather than of binding judgments; for this reason, Mesopotamian legal documents often include a promise that the settlement accepted will not be challenged in the future. The practice of going from one judge to another, which has been reported, resembles the modern appeals system, except that it was unofficial. Thus, the question whether ancient Israel had a centralized judicial system (discussed by Macholz and Whitelam, among others) needs to be rephrased; undoubtedly, a judgment by a king (or by a figure like Samuel) had higher prestige and came with more social pressure toward acceptance than did the verdicts of neighborhood judges. (Even a king's settlement could sometimes be rejected; see 1 Kgs 3:25–27 [cf. 1 Sam 14:45; 22.17 for criminal situations], *pace* Liedke:89).

[26] In most societies with a *lex talionis*, it represents a theoretical structure which in practice is "composed"; rabbinic tradition supports an interpretation. Composition is prohibited for murder (Num 35:31); by implication, it is left open for most other cases.

[27] Action theory has formed an important branch of philosophy for several decades; it can be understood as a subdivision of the theory of causality, fundamental for which is (or should be) the notion of responsibility, with various practical consequences. Specifically, from among the many factors that enter into a particular event, a causal attribution selects one or more as their human or nonhuman cause, to furnish the basis of such a response as punishment (for a human bad act), gratitude (for a human or divine good deed), remedy (for an undesirable causation generally), or utilization in the future (for desirable causation); cf Jaegwon Kim in Sosa:194. A full analysis of what is here symbolized by C and D would require attention to several components, including > (consequence).

[28] This right appears expressly in regard to punitive actions that can be composed, as in *lex talionis* (see above, note 26) and in cases of adultery (for which a killing of the offending persons by the husband is permitted when they are caught in the act [cf. Deut 22:22; Prov 6:31; and McKeating for further data]). Uncomposed, these penalties lie on the border of civil law.

²⁹ That the correspondence has a rational aspect (similarly, Levenson) is reflected in motive clauses, which cannot be adequately discussed here. (Quinn:83, utilizing deontic logic in creating a model that equates what is required with God's will, leaves open the possibility of a complex analysis, which may take account of God's character).

³⁰ If fullness of being is a fundamental value, one should reduce pain, not so much directly as indirectly through the removal of the sources of pain. The change brought about by positive feedback tends to be destructive of a given order, unless the latter is conserved by negative feedback. Only together do these two forms readily lead to a richer structure. How such fullness can be analyzed in terms of communication (including information) theory has been indicated in Buss, 1979:14-15, 19-20.

WORKS CITED

Appel, Gersion
    1975   *A Philosophy of Mizvot*. New York: KTAV.

Aqvist, Lennart
    1984   "Deontic Logic." Pp. 605-714 in *Handbook of Philosophical Logic*, II. Ed. D. Gabbay and F. Guenther. Dordrecht: Reidel

Bailey, Lloyd R.
    1987   *Capital Punishment*. Nashville: Abingdon Press.

Barth, Karl
    1946   *Kirchliche Dogmatik*. II/2. Zürich: Zollikon.

Berman, Harold J.
    1974   *The Interaction of Law and Religion*. Nashville: Abingdon Press.

Black, Donald
    1976   *The Behavior of Law*. New York: Academic Press.

Bond, E. J.
    1983   *Reason and Value*. Cambridge: Cambridge University Press.

Brunner, Emil
    1932   *Das Gebot und die Ordnungen*. Tübingen: Mohr.

Buss, Martin J.
    1977   "The Distinction Between Civil and Criminal Law in Ancient Israel." Pp. 51-62 in *Proceedings of the Sixth World Congress of Jewish Studies* I. Jerusalem: Academic Press.
    1979   "Understanding Communication." Pp. 3-44 in *Encounter With The Text*. Ed. M. Buss. Philadelphia: Fortress Press.

Casteñeda, Hector-Neri
    1977   "Perception, Belief, and the Structure of Physical Objects of Consciousness." *Synthese* 35:285-351.

Chellas, Brian F.
    1980   *Modal Logic*. Cambridge: Cambridge University Press.

Davis, J. W., et al., eds.
1969   *Philosophical Logic.* Dordrecht: Reidel.
Donagan, Alan
1977   *The Theory of Morality.* Chicago: University of Chicago Press.
Erikson, Erik H.
1964   *Insight and Responsibility.* New York: Norton.
Falk, Ze'ev W.
1981   *Law and Religion: The Jewish Experience.* Jerusalem: Mesharim.
Garcia Maynez, Eduardo
1953   *Los principios de la Ontologia formal del Derecho y su expresión simbólica.* México: Imprenta Universitaria.
Gewirth, Alan
1978   *Reason and Morality.* Chicago: University of Chicago Press
Greengus, Samuel
1987   "Israelite Law: Criminal Law." Pp. 475–78 in *The Encyclopedia of Religion.* Mircea Eliade, ed. New York: Macmillan.
Griffin, David Ray
1980   "The Holy, Necessary Goodness, and Morality." *JRelS* 8:330–49.
Habermas, Jürgen
1975   *Legitimation Crisis.* Boston: Beacon Press.
Hart, H. L. A.
1961   *The Concept of Law.* Oxford: Clarendon Press.
Hilpinen, Risto, ed.
1971   *Deontic Logic: Introductory and Systematic Readings.* Dordrecht: Reidel.
Kant, Immanuel
1788   *Kritik der praktischen Vernunft.* Riga: J. F. Hartknoch.
Kalinowski, Georges
1972   *Einführung in die Normenlogik.* Frankfurt a. M.: Athenäum.
Lampe, Ernst-Joachim
1970   *Juristische Semantik.* Bad Hamburg: Gehlen.
Lenk, Hans, ed.
1974   *Normenlogik.* Munich: Dokumentation.
Lewis, Clarence Irving
1970   *Collected Papers.* Stanford, CA: Stanford University Press.
Levenson, Jon D.
1980   "The Theologies of Commandment in Biblical Israel." *HTR* 73:17–33.

Liedke, Gerhard
1971 *Gestalt und Bezeichnung alttestamentlicher Rechtssätze.* Neukirchen: Neukirchener Verlag.

Macholz, Georg Christian
1972 "Die Stellung des Königs in der israelistischen Gerichtsverfassung." *ZAW* 84:157–82.

McKeating, Henry
1979 "Sanctions Against Adultery in Ancient Israelite Society." *JSOT* 11:57–72.

Meldon, A. I., ed.
1958 *Essays in Moral Philosophy.* Seattle: University of Washington Press.

Muraoka, T.
1985 *Emphatic Words And Structures In Biblical Hebrew.* Jerusalem: Magnes Press.

Nagel, Thomas
1986 *The View From Nowhere.* New York: Oxford University Press.

Peirce, Charles Sanders
1958 *Collected Papers.* VII. Cambridge, MA: Harvard University Press.

Philipps, Lothar
1966 "Sinn und Struktur der Normlogik." *Archiv für Rechts- und Sozialphilosophie* 52:195–219.

Putnam, Hilary
1981 *Reason, Truth, and History.* Cambridge: Cambridge University Press.

Quinn, Philip L.
1978 *Divine Commands and Moral Requirements.* Oxford: Clarendon Press.

Raz, Joseph
1970 *The Concept of a Legal System.* Oxford: Clarendon Press.

Reeder, John P., Jr.
1988 *Source, Sanction, and Salvation.* Englewood Cliffs, NJ: Prentice Hall.

Russell, Bertrand
1956 *Logic and Knowledge.* London: G. Allen & Unwin.

Schechter, S.
1910 *Some Aspects of Rabbinic Theology.* New York: Macmillan.

Sosa, Ernest, ed.
  1975 *Causation and Conditionals.* New York: Oxford University Press.

Stalnaker, Robert C., and Richard H. Thomason
  1970 "A Semantic Analysis of Conditional Logic." *Theoria* 36:23–42.

Wedberg, Anders
  1951 "Some problems in the logical analysis of legal science." *Theoria* 17:246–75.

Weinberger, Ota
  1981 *Normentheorie als Grundlage der Jurisprudenz und Ethik.* Berlin: Duncker & Humblot.

Whitelaw, Keith W.
  1979 *The Just King.* Sheffield: JSOT Press.

Wilson, Robert R.
  1983 "Israel's Judicial System in the Preexilic Period." *JQR* 74:229–48.

Wright, David P.
  1987 "Deut 21:1–9 as a Rite of Elimination." *CBQ* 49:387–403.

Wright, Georg Henrik von
  1963 *Norm and Action.* London: Routledge & Kegan Paul.
  1981 "Problems and Prospects in Deontic Logic." Pp. 399–423 in *Modern Logic — A Survey.* E. Agazzi, ed. Dordrecht: Reidel.

"DIE HE SHALL SURELY DIE"
THE STRUCTURE OF HOMICIDE
IN BIBLICAL LAW

Peter Haas
Vanderbilt University

ABSTRACT

This study applies recent developments in the academic study of law, in particular structuralism and the anthropology of law, to the Pentateuchal laws of homicide. The analysis shows that the Pentateuchal laws of homicide know of two clear-cut categories and an intermediate category. The two extreme categories are: (1) premeditated murder (רצח) which is bad and produces blood-guilt, and (2) socially mandated killings (warfare, court-ordered executions) which are good and so produce no blood-guilt. In between are cases which are deemed bad, but yet produce no blood-guilt (accidental manslaughter, killing a manslayer outside the city of refuge). This structure suggests that the Pentateuchal legal system is designed to bridge the contradiction between human society's dedication to the preservation of life on the one hand, while at the same time condoning certain types of death which occur within society on the other. To cross-check this characterization of the Pentateuchal legal thought, the rules of killing animals (for food, for the altar) are examined. A similar tripartite structure is found there, confirming the preceding result.

As humanists, we are interested in knowing how people construct worlds of meaning that allow them to make sense of the cosmos. To this end, we examine any number of social and cultural phenomena which provide epistemological frames within which understanding can occur. Unfortunately, law, which is one of the most important tools available for ordering the social world, is only rarely studied with the larger humanistic agenda in mind. Why this is so is not clear to me. Possibly this reflects an innate prejudice which holds law to be the result of conscious human political activity designed to address specific problems and so not useful for the study of how larger worlds of meaning are produced. Whatever the reason, the study of law and legal systems has only gradually emerged as a full partner in the study of human civilization.

This reluctance to subject law to the systemic analysis is especially pronounced in the area of biblical law. This is no doubt due in part to the ancient idea that biblical legislation is not of human origin but reflects divine revelation. The result is that little research has been done on the structural logic of the biblical legal corpus; that is, on uncovering the systemic nature of human thought that undergirds biblical law and so the implicit meaning that it projects onto the universe. The goal of the following paper is to pursue that line of questioning. To stay within manageable bounds, I will restrict myself to a specific body of biblical law, namely, the laws of homicide.

As is clear from the above, underlying this investigation is the assumption that the rules and regulations found in Scripture comprise a systematic structuring of human social relationships which is susceptible to academic analysis and which reflects the symbolic universe of ancient Israelites. The task of the following is to discover the underlying principles, perceptions and values which stand behind the details of the law. This method depends for its part on the assumption that the contents of any legal system grow out of an inherent, although usually unarticulated, logic that operates behind overt legislative activity by influencing how individual judges and lawyers perceive —and so define and adjudicate—conflicts.

To get at this perceptual layer the following proceeds in three steps. First, it shall examine the actual laws themselves in order to adduce the meaning they held for the people whose lives and perceptions they shaped. With these meanings in hand, it is possible, second, imaginatively to reconstruct the underlying taxonomy of social relationships that characterized the legal community of Ancient Israel. On the basis of this taxonomy, we will be equipped, finally, to draw conclusions about the deep social, religious, and moral values of the community. In short, the plan is to study the laws of the biblical community in the same way one would study the legal system of any other society.[1]

For the purposes of this study, as I said earlier, I propose to examine the Scriptural laws dealing with homicide broadly conceived, that is, with all cases in which one human being kills another. Included here are such diverse interactions as warfare, murder, manslaughter (which I use here and throughout to mean non-premeditated murder) and capital punishment.

I choose this area of legal concern for two reasons. First of all, homicide offers a fairly well-defined segment of human interaction which is of manageable size. Second, and more important for the purposes of this paper, homicide, insofar as it involves human death, is fraught with symbolic meaning. That is, we can see clearly behind biblical Israel's struggle to manage homicide and the impact of fundamental values of life and death. I shall exploit this characteristic later, when it will be possible to draw conceptual links between the laws of homicide on the one hand and the elaborate system of cultic regulations governing the spilling of animal blood at the altar, on the other. This cross-reference will help throw light not only on the values structuring the perceptions of homicide in ancient Israel, but also on its cultic life as well. For these reasons, the biblical laws of homicide offer a promising area of research for helping us adduce the core values of the biblical community that generated their laws.

Interpretive Perspectives

Before proceeding, a few words should be said about the methodological presuppositions that stand behind the present inquiry. Through such a review, I hope to clarify the questions implicit in the study of law and make clear why I choose to adopt the methodological strategy that I do. I may well begin by taking note of the central debate that has developed over precisely how the variety of Scripture's laws and ruling ought to be handled. The problem is that Scripture is a collection of diverse documents written over a period of nearly a thousand years. It is not a coherent legal compendium. In fact, even a cursory reading of the Pentateuch alone seems to reveal contradictions and tensions among the laws. The initial methodological problem, then, is to determine the character of the literature and how best to approach the diversity of its materials.

One possibility, not taken here, is to assert that the text is in fact a single, coherent and essentially seamless revelation that contains no tensions, contradictions, or differences. In light of literary criticism, this claim seems untenable. In terms of scholarly, critical approaches, I think the parameters of the debate have been laid out well by Moshe Greenberg (1960). He argues that there are two basic approaches to the study of ancient law, both of which try to take seriously the literary complexity of the text (see Schreiber: 143-44). The first he calls the historical-critical method. This methodology supposes that disagreements in the law are to be reconciled by assigning different rulings to different epochs, thus resolving apparent conflicts into a series of historically or socially discrete situations.

The second method he calls commentary. This method is similar to the unified revelation noted above. While acknowledging historical change, the commentary methodology, as defined by Greenberg, asserts that the law is nonetheless unitary and noncontradictory. What we observe in the apparent diversity of Scripture's law is development and ramification, not difference and contradiction. Accordingly, apparent discrepancies are to be handled as we would imagine that the lawyers in biblical times would handle them, namely, as involving different, albeit related, cases. All can be linked together to describe a complex and evolving whole. Broadly speaking, these seem to be the options open to us in trying to analyze the meaning behind Biblical Law.

Greenberg himself chooses the commentary method as the most appropriate for studying the biblical material. Since I agree with him, it may be helpful to restate his reasons. First, he says, it takes the text as a unit seriously. This is important, in my view, because it provides an epistemological frame for studying Scripture's content. That is, if we view the final text as a truly random collation of materials, then we really cannot bring any one part into relationship with any other. If, on the one hand, we can acknowledge that the redacted whole represents some perspective on the community and its history (even if that view is that of fourth century Jerusalem priests), then we can ask how the preserved material can be understood to interrelate and be mutually reenforcing.

Greenberg's second reason for choosing this methodological approach is that it forces the scholar to understand Scriptural law in terms of its own tradition. This reason has both a positive and a negative aspect which we should keep in mind. On the one hand, it means that we must understand a Biblical law on the basis of concepts drawn from the biblical text itself, not from "imported" concepts, say from Roman law, for example. On the other hand, this claim must presuppose that, as we said earlier, the Biblical tradition from beginning to end is essentially coherent, so that conceptions in one part are ultimately not foreign to the law in another part.

It is at precisely this point that Greenberg has been subjected to severe criticism, especially by Bernard Jackson. Jackson claims that "viewing the law as an expression of underlying postulates or values of culture" (to use Greenberg's phrase), creates more methodological problems than it solves (see Schreiber:151–52). In essence, Jackson says, even if he or she treats the entire Scriptural corpus as an organic whole, the scholar still has no way of judging whether he or she is imposing some extraneous value or postulate upon the law or is truly extracting what the ancient lawyer in each case actually had in mind. An individual law is nothing more than an individual law, and imposing any larger meaning on it is already a methodological gamble. It may be of interest to compare what different examples of law have to say on the same subject, Jackson concedes, but we must not delude ourselves into thinking that we are thereby learning about the authentic meaning of a legal system.

There can be no question that Jackson's critique of Greenberg is in order. Nonetheless I shall pursue a course closer to Greenberg in that I will assume that at least in the Pentateuch we have a collection of laws close enough in overall perception that a more or less single taxonomy of legal principles and conceptions can be read out of the details of the diverse laws found there. I prefer Greenberg's "commentary" approach also because I think it is truer to the character of legal systems to treat them as unfolding more or less linearly over time rather than breaking down into discrete semiautonomous conceptual blocks. I base this assertion in large part on the concept of law evolved within Western philosophy of law. Let me explain.

The Development of the Modern Philosophy of Law

The Western academic approach to law that informs this study stands at the end of a long chain of historical development. During the European Middle Ages, law was generally held to be derived from God, either as a direct revelation as through Scripture, or through a divinely ordained intermediary such as the king. It was only in the seventeenth century that scholars of law began seriously to consider the making of law as a social activity, thus open to academic inquiry. The original impetus, which has determined much of the Western approach to law up to the present day, was to discover behind the diversity of "positive" national laws a core of basic principles and values which all law instantiates and which therefore could serve as a basis for an international law. It was a moot point as to whether such a law was rooted in a putative original human existence in the wild ("the law of the jungle") or the innate needs of the human organism.[2] What was agreed to was the conviction that the making of law was a rational activity of the human species. All law served the same goals.

This notion, however, eventually led into a conceptual *cul de sac*. By the eighteenth century, the great studies of law, such as the writings of David Hume and Baron Montesquieu's *De l'espirit des lois*, took for granted that laws and mores were human artifices. They could show in impressive detail the logical, rational basis behind even details in received law. Yet if all law were the product of reason, then it became even harder to account for the existing diversity in the laws of Europe.

Montesquieu's work ended up opening a Pandora's box of new issues. He attempted to address the problem of variety in law by asserting that diverse cultures had markedly different laws—just as they had markedly different political cultures, religions, and customs—because each by nature reflects its unique situation and environment. Thus legal corpora could be diverse and yet still equally rational since the universal reason operating behind them has to deal with different givens. It should be noted that Montesquieu was not saying that law was determined by environment; he was well aware that law was legislated. He was endeavoring simply to put legislators on alert that a good law was one that was clearly thought out in terms of the needs of the society at hand. In casting the issue this way, Montesquieu brought to the fore a question that has plagued the study of law ever since. On the one hand, laws derive from individual legislators or judges who work in particular places and particular times. On the other hand, it is generally assumed that a legal ruling is not completely contingent and idiosyncratic, but is in fact some kind of cultural trait that reflects values that transcend the individual lawyers. The relation between the subjective individual and the objective culture thus became a central concern in the study of law. This theme led subsequent theorists to draw on both romantic notions of innate cultural genius and the emerging interest in philology and evolution to account for the effect of a cultural heritage on the individual instances of law-making, even though Montesquieu himself would have rejected such linkages.[3]

This line of the Romantic and historical study of law is probably best characterized by Friedrich Karl von Savigny, one of the most eminent nineteenth century legal scholars. Writing in the wake of Napoleon's defeat when many of the formerly occupied German territories were trying to reappropriate their native legal traditions, Savigny became interested in determining precisely what was meant by "authentic" laws. His answer was that the form of a legal system is an integral part of a people's culture, just as is their language and art. It follows that law, like language and art, is at first only crudely expressed, generally as vague mores or patterned styles of behavior. More sophisticated and articulated expressions of the legal form of the culture, again like art, depended on the availability of proper tools, techniques, and appropriate cultural sophistication. This view of law, as it turned out, had a profound effect on the study of biblical law. By asserting that a culture's law always was the overt expression of a single, culturally-linked form and that changes in the surface law were merely a matter of progressively better articulation of the underlying form, it became possible to speak of biblical law as a single and uniform approach to life that enjoyed an underlying unity despite its apparent diversity.[4] Changes in any law, biblical to be included, could thus be studied scientifically as one would a living organism, identifying morphological stages in development equivalent to the biological stages of birth, maturity, and death (see Stein:60).

Thus, according to the scheme proposed by Savigny, the study of a culture's law serves two academic functions. First, it throws light on the innate genius of a people that gives overall form to the overt legal system. Second, it provides insight into the level of cultural maturity that the society has attained at any particular time.

An important adjustment of the general view of law was made in the English-speaking world by Henry Maine. Maine's contribution was to re-express the insight covered by Savigny's term *volkgeist* in terms usable by social science. In his *Ancient Law,* Maine argued that the earliest stages of a society's laws always contain in potential all of the varied expression that the law would subsequently take. This potential, Maine continues, achieves articulation bit by bit and detail by detail as working jurists in each age struggle to apply that implicit legal heritage to the needs of their society. Drawing on the English experience, Maine was deeply aware of the conscious political work that characterizes actual legislation. So for him and his followers, the creation of law was not so much the mystical unfolding of an inherent logic, as it was often seen by Savigny and his German disciples, as it was a matter of the concrete judgments of legislators facing certain political and social choices. This had the effect of tying law-making much more closely with concrete political and social realities. The result of this recasting allowed Maine to aver, along with Savigny, that the study of law reveals both the potentialities of the culture and its various stages of growth and maturity. By emphasizing the initiative of the legislator, however, Maine focused attention on the mechanism through which the "genius" of the law worked in the real world.

This growing sophistication in the study of law coincided with the emergence of serious scholarly attempts to study the phenomenon of religion in general, and concomitantly, the religion of ancient Israel. The discovery of ancient Near Eastern civilizations in the late eighteenth and early nineteenth centuries revealed the cultural context within which Scripture's law took shape. It became evident to scholars, already becoming accustomed to seeing law as a cultural emanation of the *Volk*, that the biblical law could itself be the subject of philological and historical studies. To be properly understood, they had to be placed within the context of ancient Israelite society and its broader ancient Near Eastern context.

The operative methodology was that of Savigny and Maine. Thus the biblical laws, from Abraham to Ezra, were taken to represent various stages in the single ongoing unfolding of the legal genius of the ancient Israelites. Accordingly, biblical laws were assumed to divide themselves into epochs which could, in turn, be placed within the sequence of Israelite history. What emerged was an understanding of Israelite law that began as primitive folkways at the time the Patriarchs, developed into a mature legal system under the kings, and finally degenerated into a dry legalism under the priests, a legalism that was finally broken up only by the advent of Christianity.[5] Although this approach to Biblical law gave rise to a number of historical studies, there was little concern with how the legal system functioned altogether at any one time; the focus remained decidedly on historical development through stages of cultural and religious maturity.

Since the heyday of this historical-critical study of law, our understanding of law has shifted considerably. In particular, the idea that all law everywhere undergoes the same process of development can no longer be sustained. Nor does anyone seriously propose anymore that the law at any one time is best understood on the basis of what it was earlier or what it will become at some future time. Instead, attention is now focused on the systemic nature of law, that is, on how a legal system functions within, and gives definition and order to, a society at some given point. The character of this new inquiry into law has been shaped largely by advances in anthropological theory, beginning specifically with Bronislaw Malinowski and A. R. Radcliffe-Brown. It will be helpful in understanding the approach I take here to examine the intellectual initiative of these thinkers.

The Anthropological Approach to Law

The debate between these two giants of contemporary anthropology as to the nature of law is crucial because it has established the current state of the question with which I propose to deal. In essence, both have redefined our understanding of law by placing it within a continuum made up of all the norms that control social behavior. Basic to their debate was the question as to where folk customs end and actual law begins, and so ultimately about what a study of law could tell us.

Malinowski claimed that all sanctions or norms were to be regarded as part of a single normative webbing, regardless of how formal its statement. This means that laws can never be abstracted and studied on their own; they must always be seen in light of concurrent customs, standards of etiquette, and all other guidelines. Law was thus as much an anthropological datum as were folkways and customs.

Radcliffe-Brown, on the other hand, stayed closer to traditional understandings of law, claiming that law is a distinctly political entity and so a function of formal political or social organizations. That is, he saw law not as an extension of inherited folkways, but as a sort of artificial political imposition which was somehow not an intrinsic element of the culture. Law, for him, was of historical, but not purely anthropological, interest.

An anthropology of law did emerge, but only after some conceptual clarity was achieved as to the nature of law from an anthropological perspective. A good representative here is Paul J. Bohanan. Bohanan's claim was that wherever laws come from, we can all agree that in function they must work together with other social norms. Thus while Radcliffe-Brown might be right in saying that laws are political impositions, nonetheless they must be studied in relationship to the entire network of forces that shape interrelationships within a society, *pace* Malinowski. Laws, in short, always have their implicit (if not explicit) goal to reinforce or uphold basic values and social institutions. With this foundation laid, Bohanan moved on to develop a schema for the study of law. Since law is an explicit, political attempt to resolve basic contradictions in the culture—much as myths do at a different level—the area of most interest is where new law is being generated. There areas are clearly *loci* of tensions or contradictions in the culture. So analysis must begin where laws undergo change. The questions the scholar brings to the data focus on the deficiencies of existing law: where breaches in the society's law occur, how the society identifies those breaches, and finally how the institutions of that society propose to frame resolutions.[6]

It is on the basis of this theory that Pospisil, the most eminent of current anthropologists of law, has fashioned his approach. Pospisil addressed Bohanan's questions by examining specific precepts and rulings and adducing from them the values which compelled the judge or legislator to frame matters as he or she did. That is, from the way actual disputes are identified and resolved, Pospisil claimed to be able to adduce the broader values, principles, and convictions that operate within the society. Law, for him, is understood by gradually piecing together formative social values and principles abstracted from what legal decisions were deemed to be appropriate in the society. This view, with appropriate modifications, establishes the approach that we are about to begin.

We must deviate from Bohanan and Pospisil in one major respect. Both men assumed that we would have a reasonably complete collection of actual conflicts and decisions before us from which the broader principles of the law could be adduced. This is manifestly not the case as regards the biblical material. It is in the first place not clear as to whether or not we even have actual decisions. The legal materials are just as likely to be wishful statements as to how the authors think people ought to act. Nor is it at all clear that in either case we have a complete catalog of applicable law. In fact, we probably have little more than a sampling of some of the laws governing the ancient Israelites. We thus embark on our study of Biblical law with some limitations. Because we have no choice, we will proceed under the assumption that we have a relatively complete and accurate picture of biblical laws of homicide, and that the principles and values we see operating are in fact an accurate representation of Israelite society of the time. In any case, these assumptions allow us to adduce the value system behind the legal text at hand. The historical reliability of our results is, of course, another matter, and one that I do not propose to take up here.

Even with these assumptions, it is necessary to take some steps to insure at least a modicum of coherence in our evidence. We shall also have to attempt, as far as is possible, to collect legal statements that emerge from a single time in Israelite history. This is made easy on the one hand by the fact that the laws in the Pentateuch are generally gathered into corpora, and such collections can serve to establish epistemological frames. That is, even if all that they contain are not precisely contemporaneous, we at least know that they are all simultaneous residents of a single code and so describe a single statement of law. It is necessary, however, to insure that proper boundaries exist between corpora, so that rulings of another set do not enter into, and so contaminate, our reading of the code at hand.

This is a severe problem for the study of biblical law since the boundaries and dates of the various corpora are not at all certain. For that reason, I propose to deal in this paper only with statements of law found in the Pentateuch. In this way I hope to be dealing with a single statement of the biblical law, however uneven, while avoiding dissident or alternate views, such as the priestly laws proposed by Ezekiel. I make no historical claims as to whether these really functioned as stated. I merely treat the text as a text, that is, one presentation of the laws deemed whole and complete by its compiler. I propose to examine closely this one presentation of the law so as to adduce the taxonomy that stands behind it. On the basis of this taxonomy, I hope to be able to throw light on the system of convictions behind the community of lawyers who gave us the Pentateuch.

The particular nature of the biblical material makes it necessary to deviate from Bohanan and Pospisil in another way as well. We cannot observe the law-maker or judge at work; we have before us only a text. We must therefore have a methodology that allows us to get at the values that underlie the organization of a text to replace our inability to have access to a working judge or lawyer. For such a theory, I turn to structuralism, especially for its claim to be able to uncover the underlying convictions and so ultimate meaning of a text by studying the systematic relationships that each element of the complex bears to every other element. I am basing my use of structuralism on the claim that laws (like myths or other cultural creations) are human attempts to bridge essentially unbridgeable gaps.

For Levi-Strauss, such conflicts resolved themselves into global abstract concepts such as nature vs. civilization or, ultimately, life vs. death. The same I shall argue is ultimately true of law as well. What we shall be concerned with, then, is how basic polar contradictions inherent in human social life are arranged into workable relationships by structuring social relationships in certain ways.

To take the case at hand, the laws of homicide are designed to bring into relation the apparently mutually exclusive realizations that on the one hand it is wrong for one person to kill another while on the other such acts are an inevitable part of human society, whether by design (warfare, for example), accident, or necessity (self-defense). The legal structure built over this contradiction attempts to discover the various gradations that are possible between these polar opposites and so define and then resolve intermediate possibilities. Interpreting the legal system, then, bears some analogy to the structuralist analysis of myth. We begin with the surface manifestation (a particular incident in the myth, a particular ruling in the law), uncover the basic polarity which gives it life and then relate that polarity to the larger web of intellectual concerns which give the whole field of data its shape and character. Again, for the case at hand, we hope through the details of the various priestly laws of homicide to adduce how the authors of our legal system conceived of the space between absolute murder and full respect for all human life, and how each chartered area solved its problem through certain countervailing moves.

Biblical Homicide Law

We begin our investigation with what is surely Scripture's paradigmatic statement on the matter at hand, namely the sixth commandment. The commandment—לֹא תִרְצָח in Hebrew—has been the subject of continuing controversy. The traditional English translation has been "thou shalt not kill," but this is clearly impossible. First of all, we would then have a right to expect the verb תָּמִית (kill) rather than the less common תִרְצָח. Second, if all killing of humans was hereby proscribed, we would not have the many instances in which Biblical law condones or even mandates killing. That is, if the decalogue were really understood to prohibit all homicide, we would not find juxtaposed to it rules of warfare, the requirement to impose capital punishment for certain offenses, and the rules governing blood-vengeance and cities of refuge. The sixth commandment clearly, then, is not intended to prohibit all killing of one person by another.

One classical attempt to take these problems into account has been to translate the phrase as "You shall not 'murder.'"[7] At first glance, this seems to resolve the difficulty. The death of people involved in warfare and in capital punishment is not generally understood to be murder in its usual sense of killing innocent people. In fact, Scripture is these cases uses the term תָּמִית, which has the more general meaning of killing. Thus in situations of war, capital punishment and the like, one kills the opponent without violating the sixth commandment against "murder." Yet, we must keep in mind that the verb here means something like murder, but not murder *simpliciter*.[8] As we shall presently see, there are more categories of killing operating than at first meet the eye. A facile two-part distinction between killing and murder will not serve.

To clarify further the meaning of this text, we need to turn to its social and institutional context. Our retrieval of its operative environment begins through a consideration of the institution of the blood-avenger and the corresponding establishment of cities of refuge. This legal complex, so anomalous to our way of thinking, has been the subject of considerable scholarly reflection. Some have argued that the notion of blood vengeance grew out of an older, tribal society and that its continuation into the monarchic period was at best tolerated.[9] There is even serious question as to whether or not the cities of refuge ever really functioned.[10]

Although these are indeed serious questions, I shall not deal with them here. My interest is simply in using these rules to help define homicide in its Biblical sense, since these rulings do in fact coexist with homicide law in our text. Thus, I shall confine myself to examining the rules of blood-vengeance and asylum as a tool for reconstructing the basic taxonomy which these statements of law presuppose.

Let us turn, then, to Scripture's passages dealing with the blood-avenger. Two passages in particular will hold our attention. These are Num 35:12–34 and Deut 19:3–13. Num 35:12–34 is Scripture's major statement of the laws governing homicide. We may summarize it as follows: when a person commits homicide, blood-guilt results. If the act was intentional, the murderer must be killed. This sentence is to be carried out by the appropriate relative—the blood avenger—or by court sentence. In either case, this countervailing killing does not involve further blood-guilt. If the original homicide was unintentional, however, the perpetrator may flee to an asylum—a city of refuge—where he is safe from the blood-avenger. If this manslayer is subsequently killed by the blood-avenger while in a city of refuge, the blood-avenger's act *is* deemed murder and produces blood-guilt. If the blood-avenger kills the manslayer outside the city of refuge, however, he is not deemed to have committed murder.

Before proceeding we should take note of a number of characteristics in the text. First of all, despite the difference in translation, the same word— רצח in the *qal*—is used to describe the intentional murder (35:16), the unintentional manslayer who has recourse to a city of refuge (35:12), and the (legitimated) action of the blood-avenger who catches the manslayer outside of the city of refuge (35:27). Second, it should be noted that despite the use of the same term, blood-guilt applies to each in a distinctive way: a) premeditated murder generates blood-guilt: the murderer must be put to death (35:16f.); b) accidental homicide generates blood-guilt, but with the qualification that the manslayer is protected within a city of refuge (35:22f.); c) killing the premeditated murderer, or killing the accidental manslayer outside the city of refuge generates no blood-guilt at all (35:27). Finally, we must be aware of how this term "murder" (רָצַח) is used in comparison to its linguistic neighbor הֵמִית ("kill"). הֵמִית is used to describe what we might call non-actionable killings: capital punishments and warfare, for example. These generate no blood-guilt. The death of the premeditated murderer is always described as מֵת, that is, as nonactionable death. In the case of the accidental manslaughter, however, the blood-avenger's act is רָצַח, even if done (licitly) outside the city of refuge. It is precisely here that we seem to have a crucial taxonomic tension in the law, for the blood-avenger is described linguistically as violating the sixth commandment (committing רָצַח, not הֵמִית). Such linguistic tensions in the law serve as the key for explicating the underlying taxonomy. We shall thus need to return to this distinction shortly. First, however, we must look at the second passage, Deut 19:3–6.

The concern in these verses is the state of matters before the unintentional manslayer arrives at the city of refuge. As we already know, he is in an anomalous status: Had he been tried, he would not have been sentenced to death; yet, the blood-avenger who discovers him outside the city of refuge may kill him without incurring blood-guilt. Although the act of the avenger is not termed הֵמִית, as would be the case of a court-ordained death sentence, it is also not termed רָצַח, "murder," as it was in Numbers 35. It is described in a noncommittal way as "mortal blow," seeming to confirm what we saw above, namely, that the act of the blood-avenger is not a "true" homicide. Yet the text here does seem to regard the act as some sort of homicide. The community, we are told, must establish cities of refuge in such a way that they are easily accessible, such that the above killing would not occur (19:7–10). If the blood-avenger is able to kill the unintentional manslayer because the community has not properly established cities of refuge, verse 10 seems to say, then blood-guilt is generated; but now on the community as a whole, not (merely) the blood-avenger. Although this conception of matters is new, it is certainly continuous with the taxonomy adduced from Numbers. The act of the blood-avenger outside the city of refuge is anomalous, not really murder, but not quite non-murder either.

We may now step back and review our evidence so far. What we find is that there are in fact four progressively less serious categories of homicide operating behind this body of law. The first is simple, premeditated, outright murder. In this case full blood-guilt occurs and the murderer (רֹצֵחַ) forfeits his life. The blood-avenger may kill him (יָמִית) upon encounter just as the court has a right to condemn him to death (Num 35:21). The second category involves accidental homicide. Someone has done something to cause another to die, but the death was unintentional. In this case, we are still to regard the agent as a "murderer" (רֹצֵחַ) (Num 35:25), but of a special category. He is allowed to flee to a city of refuge where he is protected from the actions of the blood-avenger. He is to remain in that city until the regnant High Priest dies (we shall return to this detail in a moment). So while his crime is murder, it is not treated as full murder; he does not incur unconditional blood-guilt, for he has the city of asylum available.

The third category is the most problematic and will be the key to our understanding of the operative taxonomy. It involves the anomalous case in which the non-premeditated manslayer, who has the city of refuge available, is nonetheless killed by the blood-avenger outside a city of refuge. As we have seen, this act of blood-vengeance is not a full murder, but neither is it fully condoned. It either involves no blood-guilt (Numbers) or involves blood-guilt only in a general unfocused way (Deuteronomy). This same category of murder seems to apply as well to the court which passes a death sentence. The convict is "murdered" but the court members apparently incur no blood-guilt (Num 35:30). The fourth consists of those cases of fully legitimated killing: court ordered executions (see Exod 21:12–37), or the death of an enemy in battle. All of these are termed מוּת ("death").

We can sum our results in chart form:

	IMPERSONAL	PERSONAL
no blood-guilt	killing (הֵמִית)	killing manslayer outside asylum
blood-guilt	unintended manslaughter	premeditated murder (רָצַח)

Let us take the two extreme cases first. These are located in the upper left- and lower-right hand corners. In the upper left is mandated killing, such as warfare, capital punishment, and the like. These acts are impersonal, being an extension of social policy. In consonance with this view, the individual perpetrators incur no blood-guilt. They act merely as agents of the society as a whole. At the lower right is the opposite possibility, namely premeditated murder. This mode of killing is not an extension of social policy, but is a matter of purely personal initiative. Such an act, as we have seen, generates full blood-guilt.

Between these two extremes we now find two mediating positions. In the lower left we have unintended manslaughter. This act bears some similarity to straight murder: one individual is directly responsible for the death of another. Yet unintended manslaughter shares some similarities with sanctioned killings, as well, in that the death flowed out of what was otherwise a legally tolerated social encounter. Since the act fits neither prior category exactly—it is not murder *simpliciter* nor is it socially sanctioned—it incurs a sort of qualified blood-guilt. The manslayer is not automatically condemned to death (reflecting the otherwise legitimate nature of the deed), but is subject to a kind of social death (temporary exile, reflecting the fact that a homicide did occur).

The fourth category (upper right) occupies a similar mediating position. In this case, we recall, the blood-avenger finds the manslayer outside the city of refuge and kills him there. This act is in a mediating position, I submit, because of the status of the victim. The manslayer, as we have just seen, has incurred blood-guilt, but of a qualified sort. He is to suffer exile, not death. The blood-avenger's act of killing the manslayer has elements then both of socially tolerated killing (insofar as the victim as incurred blood-guilt) and of murder (insofar as the manslayer's blood-guilt was qualified). Our text signals this anomalous situation by calling the killing itself "murder" (רָצַח) but ascribing to it no farther blood-guilt.

We may sum up at this point by saying that our considerations have revealed three categories of killing: 1) warranted killings which are not deemed murders and which generate no blood-guilt. This category includes the killing of people who pose a direct threat to the community (military enemies, murderers) and who are killed by the directly affected party; 2) Premeditated homicides, which are labeled murder, are understood to generate blood-guilt for the perpetrator and are proscribed by the sixth commandment; 3) Mediating cases, which are generally labelled "murder" but are understood not to generate complete blood-guilt. Such appears to be the taxonomy of human killing implicit in these laws.

As we noted earlier in this paper, anthropologists of law have come to view as critical those areas in which the law apparently has gaps or tensions. The entire structure of intermediate categories of homicide, which generate the complex rules of cities of refuge, appears to be one such area. I thus want to look briefly at the character of this intermediate category which biblical law has constructed. My theory is that the way this gap has been defined and resolved will lead us more deeply into the structuring logic of the biblical legal system behind the texts at hand. Again insights from structuralist analyses will be helpful. Structuralist analysis claims that a pattern of response found in one area of culture is not limited to that one area but reflects a pattern of thinking that should be found across the culture. This feature, it is claimed, offers an opportunity for cross-checking the results achieved in one area. Thus the results we have achieved from our analysis of the biblical laws of homicide can be checked against other, neighboring areas of ancient Israelite law. If our first result is accurate, we should expect to find confirming evidence in contiguous legal topics; if it needs refinement, contiguous areas of law should point to the direction we need to move.

Our work on the laws of homicide is not complete, then, until we have made at least a preliminary probe of a related area of law. For this purpose, I choose the cultic laws of ritual sacrifice. As we shall see, these laws relating to the altar do, in fact, bear some structural similarities with the laws on homicide. This being the case, they help throw light on the pattern of thought behind the mediating taxa of homicide we have just isolated and identified.

Cross-Checking: The Laws of Sacrifice

Our beginning point will be the curious rule bound up with the mediating taxon that a manslayer who is able to take asylum in one of the cities of refuge must remain there until the reigning high priest dies. On the surface this requirement seems completely out of context. We would expect that the manslayer would have to stay in the asylum the rest of his life, or until the death of the principal blood-avenger or the like. Instead, we find that this expiation is linked with the life of the priest. This association, I argue, makes sense within the larger structure of the taxonomy of homicide and, as we shall see, by the role of the priests in the other major corpus of killing-legislation, the rules of the altar. In other words, the role of the priest as regards the city of refuge relates directly to a larger conception of murder as blood-spilling in the overall scheme of Israel's religious life.[11]

We go back to a contrast drawn earlier between mandated killings and absolute murders. Mandated killings are not only tolerated but are deemed necessary for the community's survival. In fact, we might argue, they are deemed acceptable (i.e., not generating blood-guilt) precisely because they are related to the welfare or survival of the community. On the other hand, prohibited killings, premeditated murder for example, are deemed highly dangerous to the community. Here the killing has the exactly opposite effect, it threatens the existence of the community. In fact such wantonly spilled blood is so intolerable that Scripture declares that if it goes unrequited the land will simply "vomit" out its inhabitants. So while in the first case it is the killing itself which furthers the survival of the community, in this other case it is the spilled blood which is intolerable and, in fact, its expiation which promotes communal survival.

This opposition illuminates a significant fact which will play a role in the interpretation to follow. What is clear from the above is that the spilling of human blood *per se* is not bad or polluting. In certain cases, as we have seen, the spilling of human blood is mandated. Taboo applies only if the blood is spilled in the wrong way, or more accurately, on the wrong occasion. It is this wrong, uncontrolled spilling of blood that violates the holy status of the community.

This is powerfully illustrated by the fact that, in a curious transformational shift, such wrongly-spilled blood is rendered harmless only by the spilling of *more* blood, albeit now in a tightly controlled, almost ritualistic way. This offers in many ways a parallel to the ceremonies and taboos surrounding the spilling of animal blood for food and for the use of the altar. It goes beyond the limits of this paper to discuss that system in detail, but a review of its major features will help make clear the intimate conjunction between Scripture's laws of homicide and the broader system of killing that characterizes its view of the sacred in general.

In brief outline, we can regard the shedding of animal blood in a number of different contexts which together describe a taxonomy of the holy parallel to that of homicide. At one extreme comes animals which have died out in nature, whether violently or through disease. Their deaths are completely random and uncontrolled. Such animals may never be eaten, and their remains render any priest who touches them unable to approach the altar. This finds it closest analog to premeditated murder. In both cases we have a death that is highly taboo within the human economy. Each generates a pollution that can be neutralized only by the shedding of countervailing blood—that of the murderer, or that of an animal brought as part of the purification process. Needless to say, the countervailing action must be accomplished in the proper way so that it mitigates the prior pollution and does not add to it. Thus the death of the murderer must be at the hands of the appropriate blood-avenger or less ideally at the hands of a duly constituted court acting as the blood-avenger's surrogate. Such a spilling of human blood, as we have seen, does not produce further blood-guilt, just as slaughtering a beast at the altar does not render the priest ritually unclean.

At the other extreme, we have the slaughter of animals at the altar. These types of killing are not only non-polluting, but are necessary for the community's survival.[12] The opposition is especially clear as regards the priest's relationship to the carcass of the sacrificed animal. Now, the priest may not only touch the carcass and its blood, but is in fact commanded to do so. In both cases, of course, these acts of "beneficial" killing must be done properly, and only through authorized individuals or agencies.

In a further parallel, we also have a mediating position as regards the killing of animals. Between prohibited meat (dying in nature) and sacrificial meat (highly taboo), we have animals that are killed in towns and villages of Israel for use as food. These animals occupy an intermediate status: they may, of course, be eaten, but only if their killing has been accompanied by certain rituals to prevent religious pollution: the blood must be buried properly, for example. We thus find an intermediate category between natural death and sacrifice. Like the mediating category of homicide, such killings are potentially polluting but may be ritualistically rendered tolerable. They are rendered tolerable because they are a foreseeable and predictable part of human society. Neither random (murder, natural death) nor mandated (capital punishment, sacrifice), such killings must be taken into account and surrounded with appropriate ritual.

When we place the problem of homicide within the larger matrix of ancient Israel's conception of the dangers of shedding blood, the connection between the high priest and the city of refuge becomes apparent. Homicide, we now see, is a ritual (and not merely a criminal) offense. The manslayer has caused polluting blood to be spilled upon the holy land. However, as long as he is in asylum, his blood may not be spilled to create the countervailing expiation. In fact, his murder there would only create further pollution. The result is that the pollution of the land created by the original murder remains unaddressed. The response of the legal system has been to fashion an intermediate status between life and death, namely exile.[13] Since the ultimate focus of the holiness of the people is the anointed priesthood at the altar, it is the high priest who remains most symbolically compromised by the wrongly spilled blood. Maybe it is for that reason that the manslayer remains in his (or her) liminal status while that high priest is still alive. It is as if the priest's death removes the remaining symbolic locus of offense, opening the way for the offender to return to the full community.

The Priestly Worldview

The structure of the Israelites' response to homicide, and its close conceptual relationship with animal death, illuminates some deeper, subterranean elements of the priestly view of the world and people's place within it. In this last section of the paper I wish to make some suggestions as to what that might be. My results must, of course, be tentative given the narrow base of our probe. Nonetheless, it may be worthwhile speculating on the broader vistas the above approach promises to open. Hopefully this in turn will allow us to come to a more complete understanding of the rules of homicide and how they function in terms of the larger organizing perceptions of the society as a whole, of which this set of rules comprises but a subsection.

Basic to the Israelite approach to the world seems to be a deep fascination with the interrelationship between death on the one hand and the ongoing life of people in the community on the other. Death of course is the great destroyer; it undoes everything that the community is dedicated to preserving. Ironically, however, without death there could be no community. The sacrificial cult seems to me to make this point eloquently. To live people must eat, and to eat they must produce death. To sustain their lives, people must eat dead things. The problem then is not to avoid death, an impossibility in any case, but to manage death so that its potency enhances, or at least does not threaten, the community. Thus it seems to me that death that occurs randomly and beyond the bounds of human society is not regarded as ontologically threatening. On the other hand, death brought about within and by the mechanisms of human society is deemed laden with danger, and so is surrounded with ritual and taboo. Thus, purposeful (that is, beneficial) death may occur at human hands, but only according to certain prescribed limits and rituals.

Homicide, however, is another matter. Here we are confronted with humanly induced death that results from the very workings of human society and economy. Such death is an extension of human activity, whether willed or not. It is at this point, when it enters the circle of human activity, that death becomes dangerously potent and so must be (ritualistically) addressed. The point of killing the premeditated murderer or exiling the manslayer to a city of refuge is thus not to be understood in our terms as a kind of punishment or even retribution for the commission of a crime. Rather, these responses are mechanisms for addressing a conceptual disharmony that has been introduced into the human economy, namely, death produced as a direct result of communal life. The need is symbolically to alleviate or neutralize the resulting sense of pollution and reestablish the community's integrity and self-understanding as a locus of holiness and life.

This survey has been undertaken to test a simple proposition, namely, that legal codes, in their details, are symbolic attempts to work out in concrete behavioral terms the implications of deeply held values and principles. Because of its ultimately structured character, the legal heritage of a community possesses at any one time a coherence and logic that is recoverable. The study accomplished above shows this to be the case for the biblical laws of homicide. What a probe such as ours aims to reveal is the workings of the human mind as it struggles to create a coherent and systematic response to the chaos and disorder of normal human social intercourse. The laws before us show the strategic moves of one such response. It goes without saying that other responses were possible; matters need not have worked out as they did. What we have seen is that under the disparate and seemingly arbitrary character of the Priestly law of homicide there lies an organizing logic that itself rests on a deep conviction as to the nature of life and death.

The above is but a modest probe into the broad expanse of biblical law. We have looked at but one somewhat artificially delimited theme in only one layer of the biblical jurisprudential heritage. A broader program of study, both synchronically (other elements of Pentateuchal law) and diachronically (what preceded and followed these writings) will fill out the broader perspectives that characterize ancient Israelite society. What has been accomplished here, it is hoped, is a demonstration of the possibilities that a humanistic study of biblical law holds for our understanding of Israelite society, and so for our understanding of Israelite society and religion, and beyond that for our understanding of how peoples attempt to achieve order and holiness in their lives and societies.

NOTES

1 An excellent example of this method is Pospisil. As an anthropologist, Pospisil deals with "tribal" or "folk" law. Nonetheless his treatment of such law as a system for actualizing the implicit values of a culture is a model for the work undertaken here.

2 The former view is that of Hugo Grotius in 1625. The later view is represented by Samuel Pufendorf 1672. See the discussion of both men in Peter Stein (3f.).

3 As evidence of Montesquieu's lack of sympathy with such theories, Peter Stein (17–18) points to Montesquieu's failure to cite the work of his contemporary fellow townsman J. F. Lafitau, whose *Moeurs des savages Ameriquains compares aux moeurs de premiers temps* showed that "savage" American Indian and "classical" Greek civilizations shared much in common.

4 By this Savigny meant something different than did Montesquieu, although the language is similar. Montesquieu related law to the very concrete and physical aspects of a society: climate, geography, and the life. Savigny, true to his Romantic context, saw the cultural genius in much more abstract terms.

5 Julius Wellhausen (1869) used legal data as part of his argument for arranging the pre-Pentateuchal documents as he did.

6 A brief and somewhat superficial review of these major positions may be found in Robert M. Rich (118ff.)

7 This is also how the matter is treated in the Septuagint, employing the Greek φονευω. Curiously, this same Greek word appears in the NT, but then is translated into English again as "kill."

8 For a discussion of the verbal form of the command, see Stamm and Andrew:98–99.

9 The idea here is that murder was originally considered a private matter, to be settled among the parties involved. The introduction of asyla was a later attempt to bring murder under public control. On this see, for example, Merz (88ff.). A more recent study along these lines is McKeating (46–68). On the other hand, Martin Buss (51–52) argues that in fact the transfer was never made, and that murder continued to be an essentially private matter.

10 Despite these uncertainties, several scholars have seen development within the law of asylum, suggesting that the law did indeed function, at least enough to require updating so as to take account of more recent changes. See, for example, Greenberg (1959:125–32) and Milgrom (278–310).

11 Other scholars have of course linked this rule regarding the high priest to the religious meaning of spilled blood. See, for example, Greenberg (1959:129–30).

12 The outstanding exception here is the killing of the Red Heifer which does in fact render those involved ritually impure. The case of the Red Heifer bears its own structural relationship to the rest of the sacrificial offerings, as shown, for example, by J. Neusner (1976:180–85, and 1981:55–65).

13 On parallels between the cities of refuge and Greek notions of banishment or exile, see Greenberg, 1959:128–29. Actual banishment outside the Land entirely was apparently not seen as a viable alternative, since this would mean, in effect, removing the offender from the worship of God and causing him to be an idolater. This would not work if his ultimate destiny is to return to the community.

WORKS CITED

Buss, Martin
    1977   "The Distinction Between Civil and Criminal Law in Ancient Israel." Pp. 51–62 in *Proceedings of the Sixth World Congress of Jewish Studies I*. Jerusalem: Academic Press.

Greenberg, Moshe
    1959   "The Biblical Conception of Asylum," *JBL* 78:125–32.
    1960   "Some Postulates of Biblical Criminal Law." Pp. 5–28 in *Yehezkel Kaufmann Jubilee Volume*. Ed. M. Haran. Jerusalem: Magnes Press.

Grotius, Hugo
    1625   *De iure belli ac pacis*.

Jackson, Bernard S.
    1975   "Reflections on Biblical Criminal Law." Pp. 25–63 in *Essays in Jewish and Comparative Legal History*. Leiden: Brill.

McKeating, Henry
    1975   "The Development of the Law on Homicide in Ancient Israel." *VT* 26:46–68.

Merz, E.
    1916   "Die Blutrache bei den Israeliten." *Beiträge zur Wissenschaft des Altentestament XX*. Leipzig.

Milgrom, Jacob
    1981   "Sancta Contagion and Altar/City Asylum." *VTSup* 32:278–310.

Neusner, Jacob
    1976   *A History of the Mishnaic Law of Purity X*. Leiden: Brill.
    1981   "Ritual without Myth: The Use of Law for the Study of Judaism." Pp. 55–65 in *Method and Meaning in Ancient Judaism II*. Chico, CA: Scholars Press.

Pospisil, Leopold
    1971   *Anthropology of Law: A Comparative Approach*. New York: Harper & Row.

Pufendorf, Samuel
    1672   *De iure naturae et gentium*.

Rich, Robert M.
    1978   *The Sociology of Law*. Washington: UPA.

Schreiber, Aaron M.
    1979   *Jewish Law and Decision-Making*. Philadelphia: Temple University.

Stamm, J. J. and M. E. Andrew
   1967   *The Ten Commandments in Recent Research*. Studies in Biblical Theology 2. 2d series. Napier: Allenson.

Stein, Peter
   1980   *Legal Evolution*. Cambridge: Cambridge University Press.

Wellhausen, Julius
   1957   *Prolegomena to the History of Ancient Israel*. 4th ed. Cleveland and New York: Meridian.

LAW AND PHILOSOPHY:
THE CASE OF SEX IN THE BIBLE[1]

Tikva Frymer-Kensky
Reconstructionist Rabbinical College

ABSTRACT

The biblical God does not model sex, is not the patron of sexual behavior, and is not even recorded as the guarantor of potency, and there is no other divine figure who can serve to control or mediate sex. Our only indication that the Bible considers sex a volatile, creative, and potentially chaotic force is from the laws. Sexuality was desacralized and kept as far away from the cult as possible. It was not, however, demonized, but rather harnessed to the institution of the family. Sexual intercourse outside of marriage was a serious threat to the social order. Fathers and husbands exercised primary authority over the sexuality of women, limited by the elders and the divine law itself. Within the family there were strict boundaries on permissible sex. Sexuality was a serious threat to social and cosmic boundaries, and violations of these boundaries were death-worthy offenses. Despite these inklings of biblical Israel's appreciation and anxiety about the topic, the Bible does not provide an adequate way to discuss and channel its anxieties and concerns.

For the modern scholar, ancient law offers many challenges and types of inquiry. First and foremost, of course, it demands to be studied for itself, as a legal system of a society: how are problems adjudicated, what is to be done in the case of theft, what are the nature of property rights, and so forth? Second, it is a record of the socio-economic system of that society: what are the social classes, who holds the property and how, what are the economic concerns addressed by the laws? Third, it presents questions of intellectual history: where did a given law come from, what is its relationship to other legal systems, what if any is the inner development within that society itself? And above all, it is an intellectual mirror of the philosophical principles of a given society. Through a culture's laws, we can see its values and some of its basic ideas about the world. Sometimes, our only access into the mind-set of a culture is through its laws. This is the case with sex in the Bible.

Sex is inherently problematic. At once cultural and physical, it defies categorization. In pagan religions there is a mystique, expressed through the sacred marriage ritual, in which sex has an important role in the bringing of fertility. The sacred marriage also gave rise to songs and poems that provided for the expression and celebration of sexual desire in a religious setting. Furthermore, the goddess of sexual attraction imparts a divine aspect to erotic impulse and a vocabulary to celebrate it and to mediate and diffuse the anxieties it may engender.

Sex and the Biblical God

But what about the Bible? Whatever may have been the case in empirical Israel, all the pagan sexual trappings disappear in the Hebrew Scriptures. The God of the Bible is male, which would make it difficult for him to represent the sex drive to a male. Even more, the God of Israel is only male by gender, not by sex. He is not at all phallic, and cannot represent male virility and sexual potency. Anthropomorphic biblical language uses body imagery of the arm, right hand, back, face and mouth, but God is not imagined below the waist. In Moses' vision at Mount Sinai, God covered Moses with his hand until he had passed by, and Moses saw only his back (Exod 33:23). In Elijah's vision, he saw nothing, and experienced only a "small still voice" (1 Kgs 19:12). In Isaiah's vision (chapter 6), two seraphim hid God's (or the seraphim's) "feet" (normally taken as a euphemism), and in Ezekiel's vision (chapters 1–2), there is only fire below the loins. God is asexual, or transsexual, or metasexual (depending on how we view this phenomenon); but he is never sexed.

Nor does God behave in sexual ways. God is the "husband" of Israel in the powerful marital metaphor. But there are no physical descriptions: God does not kiss, embrace, fondle, or otherwise express physical affection for Israel. By contrast, in the erotic metaphor that describes the attachment of Israel to Lady Wisdom, there is no hesitation to use a physical image, "hug her to you and she will exalt you, she will bring you honor if you embrace her" (Prov 4:8). Wisdom is clearly a woman-figure, and can be metaphorically embraced as a woman. But God is not a sexual male, and so there can be no physicality.

God could not model sexuality, hence it could not be a part of the sacred order. In order to underscore this, God also does not grant sexuality, erotic attraction, or potency. These are taken as matter-of-fact components of the universe and are not singled out as part of God's beneficence.

There is a concern to separate the sexual and the sacred. Before the initial revelation of God at Mount Sinai, Moses commanded Israel to abstain from sexual activity for three days (Exod 19:15).[2] This temporal separation between the sexual and the sacred also underlies the story of David's request for food during his days of fleeing from King Saul, in which he assures Ahimelech that his men can eat hallowed bread because they have been away from women for three days (1 Sam 21:4–5).

The priests, guardians of Israel's ongoing contact with the Holy, were to be conscientious in preserving a separation between Israel's priestly functions and attributes and any kind of sexuality. They were not celibate, a totally foreign idea, but their sexual activity had to be a model of controlled proper behavior. The unatonable wrong of Eli's sons was sleeping with the women who came to worship; for this they lost forever their own and their family's right to be priests (1 Sam 2:22–25). The priest's family also had to be chaste. His wife had to be a virgin, for he was not allowed to marry a divorcee. His daughters had a particular charge to be chaste while under their father's jurisdiction: he could not deliver his daughter into prostitution, and, should a priest's daughter be improperly sexually active, she was considered to have profaned *her father* and was to be burned.

Any sexuality was to be kept so far from temple service that even the wages of a prostitute were not to be given to a temple as a gift.[3] All hints of sexuality were kept far away from cultic life and religious experience.

The separation of sexuality and cult is also embedded in the impurity provisions of the sacral laws. Israel's impurity rules were intended to keep intact the essential divisions of human existence: holy and profane, life and death. They conveyed no moral valuation, and even doing a virtuous and societally necessary act, like burying the dead, would result in entering the impure state. There was also no danger involved in such "impurity"; the impure individual was not expected to die or to become ill. Such impurities were characterized by two major features: the major impurities (which last a week) were contagious, in that all who come in contact with someone impure in this way will themselves become impure for a day. And all those who are impure are isolated ritually: they cannot come to the temple or participate in sacred rites for the duration of their impurity.[4] Under these regulations, any man who has had a sexual emission, or anybody who has engaged in sexual intercourse must wash and will nevertheless be ritually impure until that evening (Lev 15:16–18). In this way, there was a marked temporal division between engaging in sexual activity and coming into the domain of the sacred.[5]

Control of Sexual Action by Law

Sexuality has been desacralized. It has not be demonized or condemned. On the contrary, it is not given sufficient status and importance to accord it a conscious valuation, even a negative one. It is talked about (or, most often, not talked about) as part of the social realm, as a question of societal regulation. The proper sphere for considering or mentioning sexuality was the law. The ideal state of existence envisioned by the Bible is marriage.[6] The monogamous nuclear family was established by God at the very beginning of human existence: "therefore a man leaves his father and mother and cleaves to his wife and they become one flesh" (Gen 2:24). Furthermore, "he who finds a wife, he finds a good thing and gets favor from the Lord" (Prov 18:22).[7] Within this marital structure, sexuality is not only permitted: it is encouraged. In God's description of life in the real world, he tells Eve, "your desire is for your husband, and he shall rule you" (Gen 3:16). Deuteronomy includes a provision for the exemption of a new bridegroom from campaigns for a year so that he may be free to cause his wife to rejoice (Deut 20:7, 24:5). The enjoyment of marriage is sexual as well as social:

> let your fountain be blessed;
> find joy in the wife of your youth—
> a loving doe, a graceful mountain goat,
> let her breasts satisfy you at all times;
> be infatuated with love of her always. (Prov 5:17–18)

And the wise man is encouraged to enjoy his marital sexuality.

Sexuality has a place in the social order in that it bonds and creates the family. The sex laws seek to control sexual behavior by delineating the proper parameters of sexual activity—those relationships and time in which it is permissible. Sexual behavior was not free. Despite the indubitable double standard in which adultery means sex with a married woman, men were also limited by the sex laws. In the case of homosexuality, men were more bound than women, since homosexuality was considered a major threat requiring the death penalty (whether real or threatened) and lesbian sex was not a matter of concern. The unequal definition of adultery results from the fact that for a man to sleep with a woman who belonged to some other household threatened the definition of "household" and "family"; for a married man to sleep with an unattached woman is not mentioned as an item of concern, and the very existence of prostitutes indicates that there were women with whom a man (married or unmarried) could have sexual experiences. This was not an unusual definition of adultery, and it has been suggested that this unevenness is the essence of male control over female sexuality, and that possibly it demonstrates a desire to be certain of paternity. Within Israel this treatment of adultery is not examined; it is part of Israel's inheritance from the ancient Near East and, like slavery and other elements of social structure, it is never questioned in the Bible.

The Pentateuchal laws also rule on sexual intercourse with a girl still living in her father's house, at which time she is expected to be chaste. According to Exod 22:15–16, if a man seduced an unbetrothed girl he had to marry her; he has engendered an obligation that he cannot refuse, and must, moreover, offer the customary brideprice. Her father had the option to refuse her to him, in which case the seducer must pay a full virgin's brideprice. The assumption in this rule is that the father has the full determination of his daughter's sexuality, a situation also assumed in the two horrible tales of the abuse of this right, Lot's offering of his daughters to the men of Sodom (Genesis 18–19) and the man of Gibeah's offering of his daughter and the Levite's concubine to the men of Gibeah (Judges 19). These men were attempting to cope with an emergency situation in which they felt their lives at risk, but the narrative considers them within their rights to offer their daughters, and Lot, in particular, is considered the one righteous man in Sodom.

The obligation a girl had to remain chaste while in her father's house is underscored in Deut 22:20ff., which prescribes that a bride whose new husband finds her not to be a virgin is to be stoned, because "she did a shameful thing in Israel, committing fornication while under her father's authority." There is good reason to suspect that this law was not expected to be followed. According to the procedure laid out in Deut 22:13–14, after the accusation, the case was brought before the elders at the gate, and the parents of the girl produced the sheet to prove that she was a virgin; once they did this, the man was flogged, fined, and lost his rights to divorce her in the future. Since the parents had plenty to time to find blood for the sheets, it is unlikely that a bridegroom would make such a charge; if he disliked the girl he could divorce her. If he nevertheless made such a charge, she and her family would have to be very ignorant not to fake the blood. But the law certainly lays down a theoretical principle very important to Israel, viz., that a girl was expected to be chaste while in her father's house. Stoning, moreover, is a very special penalty, reserved for those offenses which completely upset the hierarchical arrangements of the cosmos. In these cases, the entire community is threatened and endangered, and the entire community serves as the executioner.[8]

Stoning is also prescribed when a man comes upon a betrothed woman in town; in this case both are stoned; the girl because she did not cry for help (which would have been heard, since they were in town) and the man because he illicitly had sex with his neighbor's wife (Deut 22:23–24). The law assumes that the act was consensual: even though the word עִנָּה is often translated "rape," it rarely corresponds to forcible rape but rather implies the abusive treatment of someone else. In sexual contexts, it means illicit sex, sex with someone with whom one has no right to have sex.[9] The sense of the law about sex with a betrothed woman is that a girl, although still a virgin, is legally considered married to the man to whom she has been betrothed; hence the two are guilty of adultery and are deserving of death. Moreover, death by stoning is prescribed, whereas in regular adultery the penalty is death, but not by stoning. Sex with a betrothed girl is compound adultery: the rights of the future husband have been violated, and the girl has offended against her obligations to her father.[10]

There is a question as to who properly exercises control over sexuality. In Exodus, the father can refuse to grant his daughter to her seducer; and this kind of paternal control is also implied in Lot's offering his daughters and the man of Gibeah offering his. But Deuteronomy indicates that the father's rights were not all that absolute (at least by the time of Deuteronomy). In Deut 22:28–29, if a man grabs an unbetrothed girl and they are found, the man is to give the father 50 shekels, and he must marry her without the right to divorce her in the future. Unlike the comparable law in Exodus, there is not mention of the father's right to refuse to give his daughter to this marriage. The laws have superseded his discretion and now require what had once been the father's discretionary act.

Husbands also do not have limitless control over their wives' sexuality. According to Assyrian laws, a husband has a right to determine the penalty for his adulterous wife, or even to pardon her outright; his freedom is limited only by the fact that whatever he chooses to do to his wife, the same will be done to her adulterous partner. Israel also may have known of such husbandly determination, for the book of Proverbs, in warning the young man against adultery, warns him: "the fury of the husband will be passionate; he will show no pity on his day of vengeance. He will not have regard for any ransom; he will refuse your bribe, however great" (Prov 6:34-35). In the formal, scholastic formulation of the laws, however, the penalty for adultery is officially death, with no option of clemency.

Deuteronomy vests some of the control over these matters in the hands of the elders of Israel. It is their responsibility to uphold the social order and eliminate dangers to it. They try the recalcitrant son (21:18-21); they investigate the question of the bride's virginity (22:13-19); they oversee the release of a *levir* (25:7); and they perform the decapitated heifer ceremony (21:1-9).

But above all, the laws place the locus of control outside the discretion of individuals, by prescribing mandatory sentencing for certain offenses and leaving others for divine sanction. In the prohibited relationships of Leviticus 20, adultery, homosexuality, bestiality, and sex with step-mother, mother-in-law, and daughter-in-law are all to be punished by death; sex with a sister, sister-in-law, aunt, uncle's wife, and menstruant are also prohibited, but they are outside social sanctions and are to be punished by God.

The Bible defines the parameters of permissible sexuality by forbidding intolerable relationships. One may not have a sexual relationship that infringes on another family (adultery or sex with a girl still in her father's household), but within one's own family there are strong incest prohibitions, detailed in Leviticus 18 and 20, and Deuteronomy 27. One cannot have sex with father and mother, step-mother, paternal uncle[11] and his wife, and both maternal and paternal aunts.[12] In one's own generation, both sister and brother's wife are prohibited.[13] In the next generation, one's daughter-in-law, and, we presume, one's daughter[14] are prohibited, as are one's children's daughters. Furthermore, once one marries, one's wife's lineage is off limits: mother-in-law, wife's sister (while wife is alive), wife's daughters and granddaughters.

These incest laws seem particularly complex, and it has been suggested that the laws sought to include all those women who might be found in the same household in an extended family. However, mothers-in-law would not have been expected in these households and prohibitions on father's daughters is explicitly said to include those daughters born outside the household. Moreover, these laws took their final form when Israel already had nuclear households. The laws are defining and clarifying family lines. There is a sense, expressed in Genesis, that the marital bond creates a family even though there are no blood ties, and so father's wife, father's brother's wife, and brother's wife are said to be prohibited because the "nakedness" (the conventional translation of Hebrew עֶרְוָה) of the woman is tantamount to the nakedness of her husband. So too, since one's wife is also bonded to him, her bloodlines (שְׁאֵר) are parallel to his own and thereby prohibited. Sex within the family would blur family lines and relations and cause a collapse of family relations, and sex with daughter-in-law is explicitly called תֶּבֶל "mixing," in Lev 20:12.[15]

Sexuality As Danger To Boundaries

The power of sex to cross over the lines between households or blur distinctions between units of a family is an example of sex's power to dissolve categories. This is problematic on a national scale. This issue is clearly highlighted in Genesis 34, a chapter often called the "rape of Dinah," even though it is probably not about a forcible rape, and really is not a story about Dinah at all. Dinah had "gone out to see the daughters of the land."[16] Shechem saw her and lay with her, thus treating her improperly. In this way, he treated her as a whore (v 31), a woman whose consent is sufficient because her sexuality is not part of a family structure. Even though Dinah may have consented to the act, the fact that he had not spoken to her parents in advance constituted an impropriety. The integrity of the family has been threatened, and Dinah's own wishes are incidental. Shechem, who loved her, asked his father Hamor to acquire her for him as his wife. But there are implications to this, made explicit by Hamor, who not only tendered the offer, but extended it, saying to Jacob, "Intermarry with us; give your daughters to us and take our daughters for yourselves; you will dwell among us, and the land will be open before you" (34:9–10); he further says to his own fellow townsmen, "the men agree with us to dwell among us and be as one kindred," even intermingling "their cattle, substance and all their beasts." This inter-mixing was the great threat to Jacob's family. Even though the generation of Jacob's sons was the first to intermarry with the local inhabitants, they had to do so under controlled conditions in which they could remain a distinct unit. The free exercise of erotic love by Shechem threatened that type of control. There is, of course, also a concern that intermarriage with non-Israelite women would make it possible for them to influence their husbands to worship other gods (Deut 7:1–5), as reportedly happened to King Solomon. Ultimately, after the return from Babylon, when the community of Israel was small and in danger of being overwhelmed by the other people in the land, these dual concerns resulted in a ban on foreign wives during the time of Ezra.

The desire to maintain categories is also a cosmic issue. The Primeval History of Genesis, which underscores the basic features of human existence, is concerned to divide humanity from the divine realm, on the one hand, and the animal realm on the other. As humans become cultured creatures, they become more god-like, not resembling the great monotheist conception of God, but certainly like the divine beings to whom God speaks in Genesis 1–11, the בְּנֵי אֱלֹהִים. To preserve the difference between humans and divine, God takes steps to insure the ultimate mortality of humans. This difference is threatened when the בְּנֵי אֱלֹהִים find human women fair (they were, after all, created in the physical likeness of the divine beings) and begin to mate with them. To further reinforce the difference, God limited the human lifespan (Gen 6:1–4).

As a practical matter, one did not have to be overly concerned with human-divine matings. No divine beings were observed in the post-flood era seducing human women; presumably women were not successfully attributing unexpected babies to angelic intervention; and there is no record in the Bible of divine females coming to seduce the men of Israel, even in their sleep.

But the animal-human boundary was more problematic. The primeval history acknowledges a kinship between humans and animals: Genesis 1 understands God to have created the land animals on the same day as humans, and Genesis 2 records that the animals were first created as companions to Adam. After the flood, action was taken to establish a clear and hierarchical boundary between the human and animal world: humans could kill animals for food (sparing the blood), whereas no animal could kill a human without forfeiting its own life. In reality, this uncrossable boundary of human existence could be easily crossed by mating with animals. Such mating could threaten the very existence of humanity, for the blurring of borders would be a return to chaos.[17] Every legal collection strongly forbids bestiality (Exod 22:28, Lev 18:23, 20:15–16, Deut 17:21); Lev 18:23 explains that bestiality is תֶּבֶל, "(improper) mixing."

The maintaining of categories is particularly important in the priestly writings, for one of the essential priestly functions was the maintenance of the categories of existence (pure and impure, holy and profane, permissible and impermissible foods, family lines, sacred time, sacred space). But preoccupation with neatness is not limited to Leviticus; Deuteronomy also manifests this concern, prohibiting even the wearing of linsey-woolsey cloth, which combines wool from animals and linen from plants (Deut 22:9–11, cf. Lev 19:19).

Deviations from these neat categories are dangerous, and Leviticus proscribes male homosexuality under penalty of death (Lev 20:13, cf. 18:22). This extreme aversion to homosexuality is not inherited from other Near Eastern laws,[18] and must make sense in the light of biblical thought. It does not really disturb family lines, but it does blur the distinction between male and female, and this cannot be tolerated in the biblical system. Anything that smacks of homosexual blurring is similarly prohibited, such as cross-dressing (Deut 22:5).[19]

It has long been noted that lesbianism is not mentioned. This is not because these Levitical laws concern only male behavior: bestiality is explicitly specified to include both male and female interaction with beasts. But lesbianism was probably considered a trivial matter: it involved only women, with no risk of pregnancy; and, most important, it did not result in true physical "union" (by the male entering the female).

Public Interest in Control of Sex

Issues such as adultery, incest, homosexuality, and bestiality are not simply the private concerns of families. Like murder, they are treated as a national issue for, like murder, sexual abominations are thought to pollute the land. The very survival of Israel was at stake. Leviticus 18 relates that the inhabitants of the land before Israel indulged in the incestuous relations listed there, in bestiality and homosexuality and molech-worship, and that as a result the land became defiled and vomited out its inhabitants. Israel is warned against doing these same abominations: "Let not the land spew you out for defiling it, as it spewed out the nation that came before you" (Lev 18:28). Israel's right of occupation is contingent upon its care not to pollute the land with murder, illicit sex, and idolatry. The people must not only refrain from murder, they must not pollute the land by letting murderers go free or allowing accidental murderers to leave the city of refuge (Num 35:31–34) or by leaving the corpses of the executed unburied (Deut 21:22–23). So too, they must not only refrain from such illicit sex as adultery and incest, but must be careful to observe even such technical regulations as not allowing a man to remarry his divorced and since remarried wife (Deut 24:1–3, Jer 3:1–4).

The danger to the nation that ensues from murder and adultery explains the mandatory death sentence; it also clarifies two very odd biblical rituals. In the ceremony of the decapitated heifer, when a corpse is found but no one can identify the murderer, the elders of the city nearest the corpse go to a wadi and decapitate a heifer, declaring their lack of culpability and seeking to avert the blood-pollution of the land (Deut 21:1–9, see also Patai and Zevit). The second ritual is the trial of the suspected adulteress (Num 5:11–21; Frymer-Kensky 1984), which provides that whenever a husband suspects his wife he is to bring her to the temple, where she is to drink a potion made from holy water, dust from the floor of the sanctuary, and the dissolved curse words while answering "amen" to a priestly adjuration that should she be guilty the water will enter into her and cause her "belly to swell and her thigh to drop" (probably a prolapsed uterus). After this oath she returns to her husband. This ritual allowed a husband to resume marital relations after he suspected adultery. Otherwise, intercourse with a wife who had slept with another man could be expected to pollute the land in the same way as remarriage to a divorced wife who had been married in the interim.

Improper sexual activity had even greater danger than the threat to Israel's right to the land (which was certainly a serious consideration). The blurring of the categories of human existence through sexual activity was a danger to creation, for in biblical cosmology the universe is seen rather like a house of cards; if the lines are not kept neat, the whole edifice will collapse, "the foundations of the earth totter." Wrongful sexual activity can bring disaster to the world.

Conclusion

This is the great problematic of sex. The ideal of the bonded, monogamous nuclear family conveys a positive place for sexuality within the social order. But at the same time, the same sexual attraction which serves to reinforce society if it is controlled and confined within the marital system can destroy social order if allowed free rein. Sexuality itself is good, but the free exercise of sexuality is a prime example of wrongful activity. The exercise of free sexuality (particularly by the woman, who owes sexual exclusivity to the man) is the prime example of a lack of fidelity and a failure of allegiance. In time, all wrongful behavior was seen through the metaphor of sexual activity, with the result that in the prophets, particularly Hosea, Jeremiah, and Ezekiel, there is so much sexual imagery that it is hard to sort out what might be a literal depiction of too much sexual license from a metaphorical depiction of allegiance to foreign powers and other gods.

There is no coherent biblical treatment of sexuality. On the surface, sexuality is treated as a question of social control: who with whom, and when. There is only one explicit statement that sexuality is a cosmic force: "For love is fierce as death, passion is mighty as Sheol, its darts are darts of fire, a blazing flame; vast floods cannot quench love, nor rivers drown it" (Song of Songs 8:6–7). The stories of Pharaoh and Sarah, David and Bathsheba, and Amnon and Tamar show a sense that erotic attraction can cause men to abuse their superior position and strength.[20]

But all of this is inchoate and essentially inarticulate. There is no vocabulary in the Bible in which to discuss such matters, no divine image or symbolic system by which to mediate it. God does not model sex, is not the patron of sexual behavior, and is not even recorded as the guarantor of potency; and there is no other divine figure who can serve to control or mediate sex. Our only indication that the Bible considers sex as a volatile, creative, and potentially chaotic force is from the laws themselves. These laws of control reveal a sense that sexuality is not really matter-of-fact, that it is a two-edged sword: a force for bonding and a threat to the maintenance of boundaries. They cut through the silence on this topic, which we consider so important, but about which there is little explicit mention in the Bible. Through the laws we can find an inkling of biblical Israel's appreciation and anxiety about the topic of such vital concern.

The laws also reveal a great danger: when a society has such legitimate concerns about an important aspect of life, it needs a way to discuss and channel anxieties productively. This the Bible does not provide. We can see the concerns about sex expressed in the laws, but we cannot see how they were mediated, detoxified, expressed, and understood. The result is a core emptiness in the Bible's discussion of sex. This vacuum was possibly filled by folk traditions not recorded in the Bible. Ultimately, in Hellenistic times, it was displaced by the complex of anti-woman, anti-carnal ideas that had such a large impact on the development of Western religion and civilization.

NOTES

[1] For previous studies see Cosby, Dubarle, Larue, and Perry. This essay is based on my forthcoming book, *In the Wake of the Goddesses* (The Free Press: Macmillan, 1989).

[2] The point of this command is to separate the sexual from the sacred experience. This purpose is often obscured by the unfortunate male-centered wording of the passage. God is reported as having commanded that the people wash and sanctify themselves and wash their clothes, making preparations for the third day (Exod 19:10–11). When Moses relayed this to the people, he added his own command, "do not approach your wives" (Exod 19:15). By this addition Moses explains how the people are to prepare for the third day, but he adds his own perspective, suddenly erasing half the people, addressing only the men. It is interesting that the Bible records this as Moses' invention rather than God's; it sheds new light on the Deuteronomic injunction to the people not to add to the laws.

[3] On the basis of the interpretation of the term קְדֵשָׁה, "holy one," as a cult prostitute, scholars have long argued the existence of sacred prostitution in Israel, which the Bible was trying to stamp out. More recent work has indicated that there is absolutely no evidence that a קְדֵשָׁה was a prostitute, nor that any sexual rites ever existed in ancient Israel. In any event, the wages not to be vowed to the temple are those of a זוֹנָה which everyone agrees is an ordinary prostitute-for-hire, not attached to the temple.

[4] For a detailed discussion of these issues, see Frymer-Kensky (1983), Douglas. My analysis is somewhat different from that of Mary Douglas' classic study in that she does not distinguish between the "impurity" beliefs, which deal with a contagious state which is neither morally deserved nor dangerous to the individual and Israel's separate set of dangerous pollutions, a non-contagious state caused by misdeeds which bring the perpetrator into the danger of divine sanction.

[5] Menstrual taboos are also to some extent sexual taboos. In Israel, a woman was impure for seven days after the beginning of her menses. During this period, her impurity (as all impurity) was contagious, and could be contracted by anyone who touched her, or even sat in her seat. Intercourse with a menstruating woman was considered absolutely forbidden, and was sanctioned by the כרת penalty, which means the belief that one's lineage would be extirpated. The reminder in menstruation of a sexual dimension of existence would not by itself account for the seven-day duration of the impurity, however. Another element is at play, the blood and its association with death, for contact with death also results in a week-long impurity. It is noteworthy that only intercourse with a menstruant results both in temporary impurity and in the divine sanction of כרת.

⁶ That marriage was evaluated positively throughout the ancient Near East, see Lambert.

⁷ For Proverbs, see Snell. Snell notes the structural parallel to 8:33, in which Dame Wisdom says "he who finds me finds life and gets favor from the Lord."

⁸ On stoning, see Finkelstein. In addition to the two cases discussed here, stoning is used for the ox that gores a man to death (Exod 21:12–14), one who lures others into idolatry (Deut 13:7–8), the disobedient son (Deut 21:18–21), the practitioner of child sacrifice (Lev 20:3d), a sorcerer or necromancer (Lev 20:27), blasphemer (Lev 24:10–11), violator of the Sabbath (Num 15:32–35), and, by inference, the seditionist (1 Kings 21).

⁹ In the sexual uses of this root, there are instances where it means rape: in Judges 19–20, where the concubine in Gibeah was raped to death, and in the story of Amnon and Tamar, in which he is said to have overpowered her (2 Sam 13:12–13), and in Lamentations, in which the women of Zion are said to have been raped (Lam 5:11). But forcible rape is not always the issue. Some cases are ambiguous. In Deut 22:28–29, a man has grabbed an unbetrothed girl; he must marry her and not divorce her, because he has illicitly had sex with her. The same scenario is involved in the story of Dinah and Shechem (Genesis 34). There is no indication in the story that Shechem overpowered her. The issue is that she was not free to consent, and he should have approached her father first. Similarly, the man who sleeps with a menstruant (Ezek 22:10) or with his paternal sister (Ezek 22:11) is said to have "raped" her only in the sense of "statutory rape," i.e., that he had no right to have sex with her even if she consented. In Deut 21:10–13, the verb paradoxically seems to imply a failure to offer a sexual relationship. This is the case of a man who takes a captive woman as a wife. She must first spend a month in his house mourning her past; after which the man can have sex with her. If, however, he does not want her, he must emancipate rather than sell her, for he has "violated" her. He has put her in a position in which she expected to become his wife, and then has not carried through. The verb does not always have sexual connotations; in non-sexual contexts it means to treat harshly, exploitatively, and/or abusively. Sarah treated Hagar oppressively (Gen 16:6, 9); Laban warns Jacob not to treat his daughters badly (Gen 31:50). The most common subject is God, who is said to treat Israel badly (Duet 8:2, 3, 16: 2 Kgs 17;20; Isa 64:11, Nah 1:12), David and his seed (1 Kgs 11), the suffering servant (Isa 53:4), and individual sufferers (Pss 88:8, 89:23, 119:71, 75; Job 30:11). The most common victim is Israel, which is treated badly by God, by Egypt (Gen 15:13; Exod 1:11–13) and by enemies (2 Sam 7:10, Isa 60:14; Zeph 3:10; Ps 94:4; Lam 3:33).

¹⁰ In the case of actual rape, as when a man grabs the betrothed girl, the offense is capital, but only the man is culpable. Forcible rape is explicitly likened to murder, a realization that rape is a crime of aggression and violence rather than sex, and that the girl is a victim (Deut 22:25–27).

¹¹ Occasionally in these laws, a male is mentioned, which seems to indicate that the law also considers women and their permissible relations, but does not consistently list all of a female ego's choices.

¹² It is hard to know whether the omission of mother's brother means that mother's brother and his wife were permitted as being of a different family, or whether they would have been prohibited. A similar question arises with father's brother's children (first cousins) and with brother and sister's daughters. In this case it would seem that since father's brother is prohibited, brother's daughter must also be, even though it is not mentioned.

¹³ This was not always so in Israel. In Gen 20:16, Sarah and Abraham are described as having the same father by different mothers. A similar situation lies behind Tamar's entreaty to her would-be rapist paternal brother Amnon: "Speak unto the king, for he will not withhold me from thee" (2 Sam 13:13). This is not the only instance in which the patriarchal and Davidic narratives differ from later biblical law. Jacob is married to two sisters, which is not allowed in Leviticus. Jacob's and David's sons vie for inheritance position while, according to Deuteronomy, the first to be born is considered the first-born, whatever the wishes of the father.

¹⁴ The omission of daughter in the prohibited relations is another glaring omission. One might argue that since grandchildren are prohibited, children must also be, but one might

equally argue that the idea of paterfamilias was still strong enough that the laws could not absolutely prohibit a father's access to his daughter. From the expectation of virginity in unmarried daughters, however, it is clear the father-daughter incest was neither expected nor encouraged.

[15] It is also called זִמָּה in Lev 20:14, a term reserved in these laws for incest outside blood kin, applied to mother-in-law, wife's sister, wife's daughter and granddaughter.

[16] Probably a snide remark on the order of, "she asked for it."

[17] On the importance of categories in Israel, see Douglas, Frymer-Kensky 1983, and Finkelstein.

[18] Though the Sumerian laws consider an accusation of catamy as parallel to an accusation that one's wife is fornicating.

[19] Having eunuchs is not considered the same kind of blurring. A eunuch, like people with visible physical defects, could not serve in the temple. But eunuchs were found in Israel, particularly in the royal court (2 Kgs 20:17-18, Isa 56:3-4; Jer 29:2, 34:19, 38:7, 41:16).

[20] John van Seters believes this a particular motif in the Succession History and the Yahwist corpus. He also considers the concubine tales of Abner and Rizpah, and Adonijah and Abishag to be instances of this, but he does not sufficiently consider the political rather than sexual motivations of these acts. See further Blenkinsopp. I cannot agree that the emphasis is on love leading to death, though I agree with Van Seters that in none of these stories is the woman blameworthy.

WORKS CITED

Blenkinsopp, J. J.
    1966   "Theme and Motif in the Succession History (2 Sam 11:2f.) and the Yahwist Corpus." *VTSup* 15:44-57.

Cosby, Michael R.
    1985   *Sex in the Bible*. Prentice Hall: Englewood Cliffs.

Douglas, Mary
    1966   *Purity and Danger: Analysis of Concepts of Pollution and Taboo*. New York: Praeger.

Dubarle, A. M.
    1967   *Amour et fecondité dans le bible*. Privat, Toulouse.

Finkelstein, J. J.
    1981   *The Ox That Gored*. Transactions of the American Philosophical Society 71:26-29.

Frymer-Kensky, Tikva
    1983   "Purity, Pollution and Purgation in Biblical Israel." Pp. 399-414 in *The Word of the Lord Shall Go Forth. Essays in Honor of David Noel Freedman*. Ed. Carol Meyers and M. O'Connor. Philadelphia: Free Press.
    1984   "The Strange Case of the Suspected Sotah (Numbers v 11-31)." *VT* 34:11-26.

Lambert, W. G.
　1963　"Celibacy in the World's Old Proverbs." *BASOR* 169:63–64.

Larue, Gerald
　1983　*Sex and the Bible*. Prometheus: Buffalo.

Perry, Frank L.
　1982　*Sex and the Bible*. Atlanta: Christian Eduction Research Institute.

Patai, Rafael
　1939　"The 'Egla 'Arufa or the Expiation of the Polluted Land." *JQR* 30:59–69.

Snell, Daniel C.
　1987　"Notes on Love and Death in Proverbs." In *Love and Death in the Ancient Near East. Essays in Honor of Marvin H. Pope*, Ed. John Marks and Robert Good. Guilford, CT: Four Quarters Publishing Co.

Van Seters, John
　1987　"Love and Death in the Court History of David." Pp. 121–24 in *Love and Death in the Ancient Near East. Essays in Honor of Marvin H. Pope*, Ed. John Marks and Robert Good. Guilford, CT: Four Quarters Publishing Co.

Zevit, Ziony
　1976　"The 'Egla Ritual of Deuteronomy 21:1–9." *JBL* 95:377–90.

RATIONALE FOR CULTIC LAW: THE CASE OF IMPURITY

Jacob Milgrom
University of California

Anthropologists like Monica Wilson hold that at their "deepest level" ritual reveals values, which are sociocultural facts.
Turner (44)

ABSTRACT

The biblical laws of impurity have no meaning individually but combine into a symbolic system which instructs Israel to eschew death and choose life, represented by the antipodal terms טָמֵא and קָדוֹשׁ, respectively. Since the Lord, the quintessence of קָדוֹשׁ, defines Himself by moral attributes, the term טָמֵא, "impure," also connotes the negation of morality. The elimination of both ritual and moral impurity is the function of the חַטָּאת, the purification offering.

Impurity is the most pervasive factor in the cultic laws of the Bible. Physical impurity stemming from animals and humans is the exclusive subject of a major block in the book of Leviticus (11–15) and is a constant referent in the cultic laws attributed to priestly legislators (Lev 5:2–3; 7:19–21; 10:1–11; 21:1–4, 11–12; 22:3–9; Num 5:1–4; 6:6–12; 8:7; 9:1–15; 19:1–22; 31:19–24). Impurity also has a moral dimension. The חַטָּאת ("purification offering," Milgrom 1971, 1976a [= 1983a: 67–69, 75–84]) which purges the sanctuary of its physical impurity (Lev 16:16) is also prescribed for the elimination of moral impurity (Lev 16:21). Indeed, this purification offering is required whenever any of the Lord's prohibitive commandments is violated (Lev 4:2) and, according to a variant priestly tradition (Num 15:22–31), it is mandated if any commandment, permissive or prohibited, is disobeyed (Milgrom 1983b). It is therefore incumbent upon us to probe the biblical concept of impurity and, if possible, to determine its rationale.

A spate of reasons offered to explain impurities deriving from the human body (Leviticus 12–15), conveniently collected and rejected by Dillmann (520–22), are as follows: sin, esthetics, fear of demons, holiness of the sanctuary, separation of Israel, health, enhancement of priestly power. Other rationales have also been proposed. Henninger, citing Fallaize, ties the causes of impurity to moments of crisis such as birth, initiation, puberty, marriage, and death. Israel, however, would have been highly selective of this scheme since it imputed no impurity to initiation, puberty, or marriage and restricted the impurity of birth to the mother and exempted the child (Leviticus 12).

A more recent theory argues the notion of wholeness as the solution: "A bleeding or discharging body lacks wholeness" (Douglas:51). However, physical perfection is required only of priests and sacrifices (Leviticus 21–22) but not of edible animals for the laity, even when the latter enter the sacred compound. More to the mark is Dillmann's own suggestion that bodily discharges result in the weakening of one's strength and that the scale-diseased person (מְצֹרָע), in particular, exhibits a polarity between life and death. It is this insight which I now wish to explore.

Meigs comes even closer to the mark in defining impurity as "(1) substances which are perceived as decaying, carriers of substances and symbols of them; (2) in those contexts in which the substances, their carriers, or symbols are threatening to gain access to the body; (3) where the access is not desired" (313). Meig's conclusions are founded on her investigations of the Hua of New Guinea, and they are congruent with those reached in Culpepper's study of Zoroastrian practices: "All sickness and body excretions were understood to participate in death-impurity" (205) and Burton's evaluation of Nuer impurity: "The necessity of maintaining the distance between bleeding youth (undergoing initiation) and pregnant women, and between bleeding women (menstruants) and potential life (intercourse) is thus a symbolic statement of the necessity for keeping life-creation processes from potentially life-destructive forces" (530). This line of approach has also been taken by some biblical researchers (Dillmann:523; von Rad:272; Feldman:35–37; Füglister; Wenham:188). Their suggestion merits consideration.

First one must ask: Who precisely are the bearers of impurity? They are, in order of severity (to judge by their prescribed purification procedures) as follows: the scale-diseased person (מְצֹרָע, Leviticus 13–14); the parturient (Leviticus 12); the person with genital discharges (זָב/זָבָה, Lev 15:3–15, 28–30); the corpse-contaminated priest (Ezek 44:26–27); the corpse-contaminated Nazirite (Num 6:9–12); one whose impurity is prolonged (Lev 5:1–13); the corpse-contaminated lay person (Num 5:2–4; 19:1–20); the menstruant (Lev 15:19–24); the handler of the red cow, scapegoat, or burnt חַטָּאת (Num 19:7–10; Lev 16:26, 28); the emitter of semen (Lev 15:16–18); the carcass-contaminated person (Lev 11:24–40; 22:5); and the secondarily contaminated person (Lev 15; 22:4–7; Num 19:21–22; see further Milgrom 1986).

A mere glance at this list suffices to reveal that it is arbitrary and artificial. It does not focus on disease or even on disorders, if by that is meant unnatural disruptions of bodily functions. The inclusion of the parturient, menstruant, and emitter of semen contravenes such a notion. Furthermore, to judge by the high percentage of medical texts in the cuneiform documents of ancient Mesopotamia (Oppenheim:288–305), there can be no doubt that many diseases were also diagnosed, catalogued, and treated in ancient Israel. Thus, the conclusion is inescapable, that the impurities entered into the list have no intrinsic meaning in themselves but were selected because they serve a larger, overarching purpose.

It is of no small significance that the diet laws of the priestly system (Leviticus 11) which are contiguous to and inseparable from most of the bodily impurities in this list (Leviticus 12–15) are also governed by criteria, such as cud chewing and hoof splitting, which are equally arbitrary and meaningless in themselves but serve a larger, extrinsic purpose. Their purpose is this: to treat animal life as inviolable except for a few animals that may be eaten provided they are slaughtered properly and their blood is drained. The argumentation has been assembled elsewhere; a summary and reference follow forthwith:

Scripture decrees that since blood is life (Lev 17:11, 14; Deut 12:23), human blood may not be spilled and animal blood may not be ingested (Gen 9:4–6). Israel is enjoined to observe an additional safeguard: Blood of sacrificial animals must be drained on the authorized altar (Lev 17:3–5, 10–14). The blood requirement is subsequently desacralized: henceforth Israel may slaughter its meat profanely (Deut 12:15–16, 22–24). In effect, Israelites and non-Israelites are equated. All are bound by a single prohibition, to abstain from blood. The rationale is now clear. The human being must never lose sight of this fundamental tenet for a viable society: Life is inviolable; man has a right to nourishment, not to life. Hence the blood, the symbol of life, must be claimed, returned to the universe, to God (see further Milgrom 1963 [=1983a:104–18]).

Deuteronomy's concession that animals permitted for the table need no longer be sacrificed is qualified by the injunction: "You may slaughter . . . as I commanded you" (Deut 12:21), implying that there is an authorized method of slaughtering animals, presumably perfected by the priests, which early rabbinic tradition avers renders the animal unconscious with minimal suffering (see the analysis of שָׁחַט in Milgrom 1976b).

The effect of the criteria for edible quadrupeds (Lev 11:3) is to limit Israel to three domesticated species: sheep, goats, and cattle. The rationale given in the text is condensed into one term, קָדוֹשׁ, "holy" (Lev 11:44–45). Its root meaning is "withdrawal, separation." The diet laws which limit Israel's edible flesh to only a few of the animals permitted to other peoples constitutes an experiential mnemonic, confronted daily at the dining table, that Israel must separate itself from the nations. Furthermore, קָדוֹשׁ is the antonym of טָמֵא, "impure." If טָמֵא stands for death, קָדוֹשׁ must stand for the forces of life. The verb קָדַשׁ not only means "separate from" but "separate to." Since God is the quintessence of holiness and Israel is enjoined, וִהְיִיתֶם קְדֹשִׁים כִּי קָדוֹשׁ אֲנִי (יהוה) "Be you holy because I the Lord your God am holy" (Lev 11:44), Israel is therefore instructed to observe the life-giving and life-sustaining commandments of God (see further Milgrom 1988).

In sum, by reducing the choice of flesh to a few animals (Leviticus 11, Deuteronomy 14), enjoining the slaughter of even these few permissible animals in a humane way (Deut 14:21), and prohibiting the ingestion of blood and mandating its disposal upon the altar or by burial (Lev 17:10–14), Israel is presented with a unified and coherent dietary system whose underlying postulate is reverence for life, that bringing death to living things is a concession of God's grace and not a prerogative of human whim.

It is thus no accident that the laws of impure animal food (Leviticus 11) are followed by the laws of impure human secretions (Leviticus 12–15). Both are informed by the same ethical impulse, to separate the Israelites from the forces of death and "separate them to" (i.e., link them) to the forces of life. Reverting back to the bodily impurities listed above, it will be immediately apparent that they focus on just four phenomena: death, blood, semen, and scale-disease. Their common denominator is death. Blood and semen represent the forces of life; their loss, death. In the case of scale-disease this symbolism is made explicit: Aaron prays for his stricken sister, "Let her not be like a corpse" (Num 12:12). Furthermore, scale-disease is powerful enough to contaminate anyone under the same roof (derived from Lev 14:8; cf. *m. Kel.* 1:4; *m. Neg.* 13:17), and it is hardly a coincidence that it shares this feature with the corpse (Num 19:14). The wasting of the body, the common characteristic of all biblically impure skin diseases, symbolizes the death process as much as the loss of blood and semen.

Since impurity and holiness, represented respectively by the terms טָמֵא and קָדוֹשׁ, are semantic opposites, and since the quintessence and source of holiness is God, it behooves Israel to control the occurrence of impurity lest it impinge on the realm of the holy God. The forces pitted against each other in the cosmic struggle are no longer the benevolent and demonic deities who populate the mythologies of Israel's neighbors but the forces of life and death set loose by man himself through his obedience to or defiance of God's commandments.

Finally, it should be noted that the holiness of God is associated with His moral attributes (cf. Exod 34:6–7). It therefore follows that the commandments, Israel's ladder to holiness, must contain moral rungs. It is then no wonder that the quintessential program for achieving holiness, Leviticus chapter 19, is a combination of moral as well as ritual injunctions. Conversely, impurity, the opposing doctrine to holiness, cannot be expected to consist solely of physical characteristics. It must *ipso facto* impinge on the moral realm. This amalgam is achieved by the prescriptions for the חַטָּאת, the purification offering.

The effect of the חַטָּאת is comprehended by two verses: וְכִפֶּר עַל־ הַמִּטַּהֵר מִטֻּמְאָתוֹ . . . וְטָהֵר, "And he (the priest) shall effect purgation on behalf of the one who is purifying himself for his impurity . . . and he shall be pure" (Lev 14:19-20), וְכִפֶּר עָלָיו הַכֹּהֵן מֵחַטָּאתוֹ וְנִסְלַח לוֹ, "And the priest shall effect purgation on his behalf for his wrong that he may be forgiven" (Lev 4:26). The former verse deals with the final purification rites of the healed scale-diseased person "for his impurity" which polluted the sanctuary. The latter verse speaks of the purgation of the sanctuary of its impurity "for his wrong," that is, for the offerer's violation of "any of the Lord's prohibitive commandments" (Lev 4:2). The distinction between these two cases is between physically and morally generated impurity. This is not only indicated by the discrete terms for the causes of the sanctuary's pollution (טֻמְאָה versus חֵטְא) but by the use of two different verbs that describe the effect of the *kipper*-purgation: physical impurity is purified (טָהֵר); moral impurity needs to be forgiven (נִסְלַח).

Even more striking evidence is found in the provisions for Yom Kippur, the Day of Atonement. The key term in the high priest's confession over the scapegoat is עֲוֹנֹת, "iniquities" (Lev 16:21). It parallels and corresponds in importance to טֻמְאֹת, "impurities," the term which sums up the goal of the sanctuary's purgation with the חַטָּאת blood (v 16). Indeed, the only difference between the inventory of wrongs purged by the blood and those purged by the scapegoat is that "impurities" is replaced by "iniquities." Thus it is clear that the blood purges the physical impurity of the sanctuary and the scapegoat purges the moral impurity of the people. "For pollution that befalls the Temple and its sancta through wantonness, atonement is effected by the goat whose blood is sprinkled within the adytum and by the Day of Atonement; *for all other wrongs* specified in the Torah—minor or grave, wanton or inadvertent, conscious or unconscious, through commission or omission . . . the scapegoat effects atonement" (*m. Sebu.* cf. *Sipra Ahare* 5:8, italics are mine).

Two bits of evidence confirms this rabbinic insight: (1) In the purgation rite for the shrine (Lev 4:3-21), the sacrificed חַטָּאת suffices; an additional live animal is not required. Thus, the sacrificed חַטָּאת animals of Leviticus 16 also suffice to purge the sanctuary. This leaves the live goat to function in an entirely different sphere: the elimination of Israel's moral sins. (2) Two חַטָּאת offerings are prescribed for the purging of the sanctuary: a bull for the priests and a goat for the people (Lev 16:11, 15-16). Two animals are needed because the high priest must first purge the sanctuary of his and his fellow priests' impurities before he can act on behalf of the people. However, only one live goat suffices to atone both for the priests and the people. If its purpose was to carry off the sanctuary's impurities, should not the high priest have first confessed his sins and those of the priests over a live goat of his own before he could officiate over the live goat of the people? Again, the only answer can be that the live goat has nothing to do with the sanctuary's impurities but, as the text states emphatically and unambiguously, it deals with the עֲוֹנֹת "iniquities"—the moral sins of all the people, priests and laity alike.

To recapitulate, the concept of impurity in the Bible, demythologized and eviscerated of its originally demonic content, became restricted to those bodily manifestations associated with death. Israel was enjoined to shun impurity and, whenever that was not possible, to eradicate it through purificatory rituals. It was not death but life that Israel was to pursue. Hence holiness, the semantic and ideological antonym of impurity, became the goal. Holiness implied pursuing the moral values associated with the divine nature. Correspondingly, the concept of impurity was broadened to denote the violation of these moral values. Thus, impurity and holiness came to be identified with Israel's response to the totality of commandments. The priestly legists stated the matter dogmatically: "Observe my statutes and norms, for the person who does them will find life through them" (Lev 18:5). The deuteronomist exhorts in a similar vein, adding only that the choice is each person's: "I have put before you life and death, blessing and curse. Choose life" (Deut 30:19).

WORKS CITED

Burton, J. W.
    1974   "Some Nuer Notions of Purity and Danger." *Anthropos* 69:517–36.

Culpepper, E.
    1974   "Zoroastrian Menstrual Taboos." In *Women and Religion*. Ed. J. Plaskow. Missoula: Scholars Press.

Dillmann, A. and V. Ryssel
    1897   *Die Bucher Exodus und Leviticus*. KeH. 3d ed. Leipzig: Hirzel.

Douglas, M.
    1966   *Purity and Danger*. New York: Praeger.

Feldman, E.
    1977   *Biblical and Post-Biblical Defilement and Mourning*. New York: Ktav.

Füglister, N.
    1977   "Sühne durch Blut. Zur Bedeutung von Leviticus 17.11." Pp. 143–64 in *Studien zum Pentateuch* (Festschrift Kornfeld). Ed. G. Braulik. Vienna: Herder.

Henninger, J.
    1979   "Pureté et impureté. L'histoire des religions." *DBSup* 9:399–430.

Meigs, A. S.
    1978   "A Papuan Perspective on Pollution." *Man* 13:304–18.

Milgrom, J.
1963 "The Biblical Diet Laws as an Ethical System," *Int* 17:288-301 [=*Studies in Cultic Theology and Terminology* (Leiden: Brill, 1983a) 104-18].
1971 "Sin-offering or Purification-offering" *VT* 21:237-39 [=1983a *Studies in Cultic Theology and Terminology*. Leiden: Brill, 67-69].
1976a "Israel's Sanctuary: The Priestly 'Picture of Dorian Gray.'" *RB* 83:390-99 [=1983a *Studies in Cultic Theology and Terminology*. Leiden: Brill, 75-84].
1976b "Profane Slaughter and a Formulaic Key to the Composition of Deuteronomy." *HUCA* 47:1-17.
1983b "The Two Pericopes on the Purification Offering," *The Word of the Lord Shall Go Forth: Essays in Honor of David N. Freedman*. Eds. C. L. Myers and M. O'Connor. Winona Lake: Eisenbrauns:211-15.
1986 "The Priestly Impurity System." Pp. 21-27 in *Proceedings of the Ninth World Congress of Jewish Studies*. Jerusalem: Academic Press.
1988 "Ethics and Ritual: The Foundations of the Biblical Dietary Laws." *Religion and Law: Biblical, Jewish and Islamic Perspectives*. Ed. E. B. Firmage, et al. Winona Lake: Eisenbrauns.

Oppenheim, A. L.
1964 *Ancient Mesopotamia*. Chicago: University of Chicago.

von Rad, G.
1962 *Old Testament Theology*. Vol 1. New York: Harper and Row.

Turner, V.
1967 *The Forest of Symbols*. Ithaca: Cornell University Press.

Wenham, G. J.
1983 "Why Does Sexual Intercourse Defile? (Lev 15:15)." *ZAW* 95:432-34.

www.ingramcontent.com/pod-product-compliance
Lightning Source LLC
Chambersburg PA
CBHW032302150426
43195CB00008BA/550